Instant Pot

Desserts

Instant Pot

Desserts

Sweet Recipes for Your Electric Pressure Cooker

Laurel Randolph

Photographs by Rebecca Peloquin

Good Books

New York, New York

Good Books books may be purchased in bulk at special discounts for sales
promotion, corporate gifts, fund-raising, or educational purposes. Special
editions can also be created to specifications. For details, contact the Special Sales
Department, Good Books, 307 West 36th Street, 11th Floor, New York, NY 10018
or info@skyhorsepublishing.com.

Good Books is an imprint of Skyhorse Publishing, Inc.®, a Delaware corporation.

Visit our website at www.goodbooks.com

10 9 8 7 6 5 4 3 2 1

Library of Congress Cataloging-in-Publication Data is available on file.

Cover design by Daniel Brount
Cover photograph by Rebecca Peloquin

Print ISBN: 978-1-6809-9590-9
Ebook ISBN: 978-1-6809-9591-6

Printed in China

For Betty and Winston, who taught me there's always room for dessert.

Contents

Introduction

Everyone knows the Instant Pot is fantastic at cranking out soups, whole grains, and tender meat, but what about desserts? Not only can the device make top-notch cheesecakes, but it can make a whole book's worth of desserts. This book, in fact. From puddings to cakes to pies to cobblers, you can make all the included sweet treats in an electric pressure cooker with minimal extra equipment.

Other than the pure novelty of making a bundt cake in a computerized multi-cooker, there are a few good reasons for cooking desserts in an Instant Pot. Have you ever wanted dessert but couldn't justify making an entire cake for just a few people? Or have you ever made a fancy dessert for a dinner party and were stuck with way too much left over? Since everything has to fit inside the modestly-sized pot, most recipes in this book serve 8 or fewer, with many serving only 3 or 4. There's even a crème brûlée recipe for one!

Plus, while your last course is cooking away in the pot, you've got the oven and stove free for making dinner. It makes multi-tasking easy as can be and is extra handy when entertaining.

Lastly, since pressure cookers lock in moisture and heat, they create a perfect steam environment without heating up your kitchen. Most desserts require baking and can turn the whole room into an oven on a hot day. Rather than swearing off all sweets except ice cream for the summer, use the pot to make a memorable dessert.

I'll be the first to say that pressure cookers are not good for cooking everything, just like you can't make everything well in a microwave or on a stove. They are, however, excellent for making rice puddings, cheesecakes, custards, steamed cakes and pies, flans, and cobblers. You'll be surprised by the beautiful and delicious desserts that will emerge from your Instant Pot.

Terminology and Functions

If you're new to the Instant Pot, some of the terms in this book might not be familiar. Before using your pressure cooker, read the manual from cover to cover and get familiar with your appliance. When you're ready to tackle a dessert, here's a handy reference guide to refresh your memory.

- **Pressure Cook**

  Every recipe in this book is cooked using the pressure cook function. This is sometimes called "Manual" on some Instant Pot models, but they are one and the same. Most recipes cook on **high pressure**, the pot's default, while some cook at **low pressure**. Take note of which pressure level a recipe calls for and program your cooker accordingly. Note that one model of Instant Pot, the Lux, does not have a low pressure setting; whenever possible, a note is provided at the end of low pressure recipes for how to adjust.

- **Sauté**

  This is another function available on the Instant Pot and is used sparingly in this book to prep or finish a recipe. Most Instant Pots default to medium heat on the sauté function. There's no need to adjust—medium, or "normal," works for the recipes that use the sauté function in this book.

- **Natural Release**

  There are two ways you can release pressure from a pressure cooker, one being a natural release. This means the pressure naturally escapes the cooker slowly and can take anywhere from 5 minutes to over 30 minutes. I recommend turning off the Keep Warm function when your cooker has completed its pressure cooking, but you can otherwise leave it be and even unplug it. Listen for the floating valve to drop in the lid with a click, signaling the pressure has released, and then you can retrieve your dessert. For your safety, the lid will not unlock until all the pressure has been released.

- **Quick Release**

  The second option for releasing pressure is a quick release. Also known as a manual release, this requires you to open the steam release valve manually and release the pressure. You may use a quick release once the timer counts down to zero and beeps that the cook time is finished. Be careful when opening the steam release valve, and consult your manual for more safety information.

  Some recipes in this book call for a natural release for a specified amount of time and then a quick release, such as "use a natural release for 10 minutes followed by a quick release." Once your pot beeps that it is done cooking, you should set a timer for 10 minutes (per this example). After the timer goes off, release the pressure using a quick release.

- **Foil Sling**

  This is an easy-to-make, affordable tool to help you lift pans out of the cooker. See page xv for how to make a foil sling.

"Baking" in an Instant Pot

There are some aspects of "baking" in a pressure cooker unique to the device, some that are unique to steaming, and some that are universal to all baking. Here are some reminders when producing sweets from your pot.

- **Measuring**

  How you measure dry and wet ingredients can greatly impact the chemistry and, therefore, the texture and flavor of your final dessert. When measuring **flour**, use a spoon or smaller measuring cup to overfill the appropriately sized measuring cup. Then use a butter knife, with the blade turned on its side, to sweep across the top of the cup and remove excess flour. The result should be flour that has completely filled the cup and is perfectly level with the very top.

  When measuring **brown sugar**, scoop the sugar into the measuring cup and press it down, then swipe any excess off the top with a knife. When you add it to the bowl, the brown sugar will keep the shape of the measuring cup. This is what "packed" means when referring to brown sugar.

  Cornstarch and leaveners like baking soda and powder should be accurately measured at all times for best results. For wet ingredients, a liquid measure like a glass 2-cup measurement is best. Measuring cups will also work but should be filled to the brim.

- **Leaveners**

  Experienced bakers may notice that cake recipes cooked in the Instant Pot contain more than the usual amount of leaveners per volume. Because cakes are steamed in the Instant Pot, they need a little more lift to achieve a good texture. Baking powder is used frequently in the cake recipes in this book with a few also using baking soda. Note that batters with baking soda should be cooked right away and not left to sit since the reaction is immediate. That being said, all the recipes in this book were designed to be cooked right away for best results.

- **Temperature**

  Just like any dessert cookbook, there are recipes in this book that call for ingredients at room temperature or softened (like butter, eggs, and cream cheese) or cold (butter). These temperatures may seem unimportant, but they will have a real effect on the final product. Softened butter and cream cheese should be at room temperature, squishy, and no longer cold to the touch but not melted. Leaving ingredients out for at least an hour is usually sufficient to bring them to room temperature.

If you forgot to set out your butter or cream cheese before making a cake, cut into chunks and microwave for 15-second intervals at low heat. Keep a close eye on it since you do not want any of the butter to melt. Eggs can be brought to room temperature by submerging them in a lukewarm bowl of water for a few minutes.

- **Greasing and Lining Pans**

  If a recipe calls for greasing and/or lining the baking pan, do not skip this step. There's nothing worse than working hard on a dessert and it completely sticking to the pan. When greasing, use an even coating of nonstick spray all over, or use a small nub of butter to coat completely. Make sure to reach all the nooks and crannies, but don't over-grease and leave chunks of butter or pools of oil.

  Some recipes call for a parchment circle to line the bottom of the pan. For more information on how to make a parchment circle, see page xv.

- **Doneness**

  If you're used to traditional baking, it can be hard to tell when a pressure-cooked dessert is cooked through. Since no browning occurs, you have to rely on the visual indicators included in each recipe and, when appropriate, a toothpick test. For cakes, insert a toothpick or cake tester into the center (for bundt cakes, test the middle of the ring of cake, not next to the center of the pan). Try to avoid any fruit or nuts when you stick in the tester. The tester should be clean or have a few cooked crumbs attached and not be coated in wet batter.

  When steaming cakes, it's better to overcook than undercook. Since it is a moist environment, it's harder to dry out a steamed cake than when baking. If you're worried that a cake isn't thoroughly cooked, put it back in the pot for a few more minutes of cook time. (It will need to come to pressure again.)

Pot-In-Pot Cooking Basics

Many of the recipes in this book use a pressure-cooking method called "pot-in-pot." This means the food is cooked inside a container, such as a pan or ramekin, inside the Instant Pot with water underneath. It's essentially an efficient way of steaming food. Almost all pot-in-pot recipes follow the same basic steps.

1. Add at least 1 cup of water to the inner pot of the cooker. The Instant Pot needs at least 1 cup of liquid to come to pressure, and in the case of pot-in-pot cooking, that liquid is water. The recipes in this book call for 1¼ cups of water so that there is no risk of

your pot not having enough liquid to operate properly. Don't add more than 1½ cups (unless called for in the recipe) since you risk your dessert getting wet.

2. Place the steam rack included with the Instant Pot in the pot on top of the water. Depending on what pan you are using, you may need to fold down the handles so that there is enough room for the pan.

3. If needed, make a foil sling. You'll see this phrase several times in this book. A foil sling is necessary when you have to lower the handles of the steam rack to fit the pan inside or the rack handles don't reach high enough to grab. A foil sling allows you retrieve the pan from the cooker without having to dig around in a very hot, steaming pot. See page xv for how to make a foil sling.

4. Some recipes call for the pan or ramekins to be covered with aluminum foil and some do not. Be sure to follow the instructions. When removing the lid after cooking an uncovered dessert, quickly tilt and draw away the lid to avoid dripping condensation on top. If needed, you can very carefully use a piece of paper towel to dab away any excess moisture sitting on top.

Equipment

There are several recipes in this book that don't require any special equipment, including rice puddings and poached fruits that cook directly in the pot. The rest, however, require a pan, ramekins, or jars. Here's a list of all the things you'll need for successful dessert-making in the Instant Pot.

- **Steam Rack**

  All Instant Pot models come with a steam rack. Make sure you have yours handy.

- **Clean Sealing Ring**

  I recommend that everyone buys an extra silicone sealing ring for their Instant Pot. Use one for smelly dishes like chili and curry and the other for delicate items like yogurt and desserts—that way your rice pudding won't have a whiff of garlic. Extra rings can easily be bought online; just make sure the one you buy is compatible with your model of cooker.

- **7-Inch Cheesecake or Springform Pan**

  Several recipes in this cookbook are made using a 7-inch cheesecake (removable bottom) or springform pan. Any brand will work as long as a few standards are met: The pan is high-temperature safe, it actually fits inside of your cooker (the spring on some

springform pans makes them too wide), and the walls are high enough. I recommend a 7x3-inch pan. With walls that high, you won't have any leakage when dishes like cheesecakes puff up.

Note that you can often use a 7-inch cheesecake or springform pan when a recipe calls for a standard 7-inch baking pan. You'll want to line the inside of the pan tightly with aluminum foil to prevent leaks before greasing.

- **7-Inch Baking Pan**
Gooey dishes like bread pudding that are at risk of leaking out of a cheesecake pan require a 7-inch baking pan. I recommend a 7x3-inch pan for maximum versatility. These pans can be found at restaurant supply stores or ordered online. Always double check to make sure a pan fits in your cooker before purchasing.

- **6-Cup Bundt Pan**
There are some top-notch bundt cakes in this book, but you'll need a cute little 6-cup bundt pan for that. For reference, standard bundt pans are 10- or 12-cup capacity. Look for one without big handles so that it'll actually fit into your cooker. If you use a steamed pudding baking tin, you may need to adjust the cook time, since the center of the cake will be thicker without the hole found in the center of a traditional bundt pan.

- **Ramekins**
Ramekins are used in this cookbook to make individual-sized desserts like flan, pudding, and crème brûlée. Recipes call for 5-, 6-, or 7-ounce ramekins. If you're buying a set specifically for this cookbook, I'd recommend four 6-ounce ramekins. Regardless of what ramekins you use, make sure they are oven-safe and fit well in your cooker. Ramekins can be stacked, but I do not recommend stacking more than one on top. Perch it at the intersection of two or three ramekins underneath.

- **Ramekin Alternatives**
Some recipes can also be made with half-pint jars. Double check that your jars are heat-safe; some jars are made for decorative purposes and are not safe to pressure cook. Always check jars for cracks and chips before using and handle with extreme caution. There is still a chance of breakage.

Many recipes calling for ramekins can also be made with appropriately sized mugs. Don't be afraid to get creative as long as you're being safe by using heat-safe dishes and not stacking precariously. If needed, you can always cook ramekin recipes in batches.

- **Aluminum Foil**

  A roll of aluminum foil will be your best friend when using this cookbook. Many dishes need to be tightly covered when cooking in the pot, and you may need a sling for some recipes.

- **Foil Sling or Silicone Sling**

  If the steam rack's handles aren't long enough to reach above the pan you're using, or you need to fold down the rack's handles, then you'll need a sling. You can buy a silicone one online for this exact purpose, or you can easily make one with aluminum foil.

  To make a foil sling, tear off a piece of aluminum foil about two feet long. Fold it, longways, into thirds, creating a long rectangle. Place your prepared pan centered on top of the foil and grab both ends of the sling and lift them upwards. Use the sling to lift the pan and lower it into the cooker. Fold the ends of the sling over the top of the pan to ensure it won't interfere with the lid. Once done cooking, use the sling to lift the pan out of the pot. If still clean, you can leave the sling to dry and reuse it next time.

- **Parchment Paper**

  Lining the bottom of a pan with a circle of parchment paper can help ensure easy removal. When purchasing, make sure you're buying parchment paper and not wax paper.

  To make a parchment circle, unroll enough parchment to set your pan on top. Trace around the bottom of your pan with a pencil. Remove the pan and cut out the circle, cutting just inside the outline so that it will perfectly fit inside the bottom of your pan.

Recipe Considerations and Alterations

Generally speaking, big alterations to pressure-cooking recipes are not recommended. Because of the way pressure cooking works, the cook times and amount of liquid are specifically formulated to work as written. If you're an experienced Instant Potter, then you have a grasp on what can and can't be tweaked. If you're new to the gadget, I'd stick to the recipes until you get the hang of things.

For this cookbook, following the recipe is especially important. Just like with normal baking, changing things too much in a recipe can cause the chemistry to run amok, resulting in a chewy cake or a runny pudding. I've provided variations for the recipes when possible, but beyond that, you're on your own when making changes and results cannot be guaranteed. Some easy ways to make these recipes your own without changing the texture of the dish include switching out dried spices, adding a dash of flavor extract (like orange or almond), or swapping fresh fruit used as a garnish for a different variety.

If you want to adapt one of your own baked or stovetop desserts for the Instant Pot, take great care with your experimenting. It may take a few tries to get it right, and some recipes just aren't meant for pressure cooking (trust me, I've tried). If you have a recipe similar to one in this book, feel free to use my recipe as a guide to help you figure out how to scale the ingredients and the cook time. Do not overfill your pans or the pot since that will cause the cooker to malfunction.

Here are some other considerations when using this book.

- **Times**

  Each recipe includes prep time, cook time, and total time. The **prep time** includes all hands-on prep and soaking times, as well as any cooking that is not pressure cooking. The **cook time** is the pressure cook time and the number you'll program into your pot. The **total time** includes the prep time, cook time, and the time the cooker takes to come up to pressure and release pressure. This is an estimate, since your cooker may take less or more time to gain and release pressure based on a number of factors.

- **Serving Size**

  If you'd like to halve or double a recipe, use caution. Whole cakes should not be adjusted since the pan size will no longer work. Recipes that cook inside the pot should not be doubled if it will make the cooker over two-thirds full, and should not be reduced if the liquid will equal less than one cup. Ramekin recipes can sometimes be halved and it will not affect the cook time. If they are doubled, be sure to use twice the number of ramekins, and you may need to cook them in shifts.

- **Cooker Size**

  All the recipes in this book were testing in a 6-quart, standard-sized Instant Pot. Whenever possible, notes are included on how to make recipes in a 3-quart and 8-quart. Note that some recipes are not compatible with the 3-quart as written.

- **Dietary Notes**

  When appropriate, recipes are labeled as Gluten-Free, Vegan, or No Added Sugar. When the word *option* appears after any of these words, such as *Vegan option*, that means there's a note included for how to make that recipe vegan.

  Many recipes in this book are **gluten-free** (and labeled as such) or have an option to make them gluten-free. Note that all ingredients will need to be checked to make sure there are no trace amounts of gluten. Some recipes have an option for "**no added**

sugar." Read the instructions on your sugar substitute carefully when replacing sugar in a recipe to ensure the recipe does not end up too sweet.

- **Altitude**

  Pressure cookers are a great tool for cooks living at high elevation, but you'll still need to adjust the cook times a bit. The general rule is to add 5 percent to the cook time for every 1,000 feet you live above sea level.

- **Notes**

  Don't be afraid to mark up this book. There are designated spaces throughout to make your own notes about the recipes.

Cakes

Bundt Cakes
Banana-Lime Bundt Cake 3
Moist Apple Bundt Cake 5
Pineapple Rum Cake 6
Sticky Date Cake 7

Cheesecakes
Dark Chocolate Peppermint Cheesecake 10
Mango Cheesecake 13
Salted Peanut Butter Cheesecake 16
Strawberries and Cream Cheesecake 19

Classic Cakes
Classic Carrot Cake 21
Chocolate-Orange Lava Cakes 25
Dried Cherry and Pecan Fruit Cake 26
Flourless Chocolate Cake 28

Fruity Cakes
Plum Cornmeal Cake 31
Pineapple Upside Down Cake 33
Lemon-Ricotta Mini Cakes 35

Banana-Lime Bundt Cake

Serves 8

Prep Time: 15 minutes | **Cook Time:** 50 minutes | **Total Time:** 1 hour, 40 minutes

Moist, fluffy banana cake gets a little twist with the addition of lime. Zest and juice appear in the cake and icing, but it's not too tart. The cake is close enough to banana bread that it's a nice addition to a brunch spread, too.

---

2 cups all-purpose flour

1 teaspoon baking powder

1 teaspoon baking soda

½ teaspoon salt

1 stick unsalted butter (½ cup), softened

½ cup granulated sugar

⅓ cup brown sugar, packed

2 eggs, room temperature

3 very ripe bananas, mashed

2 tablespoons plain yogurt (or sour cream)

3–4 tablespoons fresh lime juice, divided

¾ cup powdered sugar

1 teaspoon vanilla extract

1 teaspoon finely grated lime zest, divided

Notes:
- Make it gluten-free by replacing the flour with your favorite gluten-free all-purpose flour mix.
- If you don't have a bundt pan, you can bake this cake in a tall 7-inch cake pan—just add 5 minutes to the cook time. Note that the cake won't yield quite as good results as using a bundt pan, but it's still delicious.

1. Add the steam rack to the pot and 1¼ cups water. Grease a 6-cup bundt pan. If needed, create a sling (see page xv)

2. In a small mixing bowl, combine the flour, baking powder, baking soda, and salt. Mix and set aside.

3. In a medium mixing bowl, beat the butter, granulated sugar, and brown sugar with an electric mixer for 2 minutes, or until creamy and fluffy. Add the eggs and beat until creamy. Add the mashed banana, yogurt, 2 tablespoons lime juice, vanilla, and ¾ teaspoon lime zest and beat just until mixed, scraping down the sides.

4. Add the flour mixture, and stir by hand just until completely combined.

5. Pour the batter into the prepared pan and smooth out to make level. Cover with aluminum foil. Place on the steam rack and secure the lid.

6. Cook at high pressure for 50 minutes and use a natural release for 30 minutes, followed by a quick release.

7. Carefully remove the pan from the pot and remove the foil. The cake should be cooked through. Let cool for about 10 minutes in the pan before turning out and cooling completely on a rack.

8. Before serving, combine the powdered sugar, 1 tablespoon lime juice, and remaining ¼ teaspoon lime zest in a small bowl and mix well. Add more lime juice as needed, a little at a time, to reach the desired consistency. Drizzle over the cake.

9. Store leftovers in an airtight container at room temperature for up to 3 days.

Gluten-free option | 8 quart: Make as written

Moist Apple Bundt Cake

Serves 8

Prep Time: 25 minutes | **Cook Time:** 40 minutes | **Total Time:** 1 hour, 40 minutes

Studded with chunks of apple and walnut, this spiced cake screams fall but tastes delicious all year long. A drizzle of reduced apple cider and brown sugar soaks into the cake after baking, infusing it with fruity flavor and keeping it moist.

---

2 cups all-purpose flour

1½ teaspoons ground cinnamon

1½ teaspoons baking powder

1 teaspoon baking soda

½ teaspoon salt

½ cup canola oil (or vegetable oil)

¾ cup granulated sugar

2 eggs, beaten

1 tablespoon molasses (or honey)

1 tablespoon fresh lemon juice

1 teaspoon vanilla extract

2½ cups peeled, small diced apple (2–3 apples)

½ cup chopped walnuts (optional)

1½ cups apple cider or apple juice

2 tablespoons brown sugar, packed

Note:
- Make it vegan by replacing the eggs with egg replacer (follow package directions).

1. Add the steam rack to the pot and 1¼ cups water. Grease a 6-cup bundt pan. If needed, create a sling (see page xv)

2. In a small mixing bowl, combine the flour, cinnamon, baking powder, baking soda, and salt. Mix and set aside.

3. In a medium mixing bowl, beat the oil, sugar, eggs, molasses, lemon, and vanilla with an electric mixer until well mixed. Scrape down the sides and add the flour mixture, mixing just until completely mixed.

4. Add diced apple and walnuts (if using), and mix by hand just until incorporated.

5. Pour the batter into the prepared pan and spread to make level. Cover with aluminum foil. Place on the steam rack and secure the lid.

6. Cook at high pressure for 40 minutes and use a natural release for 30 minutes followed by a quick release.

7. Carefully remove the pan from the pot and remove the foil. The cake should be cooked through. Let cool for about 10 minutes in the pan before turning out and onto a rack.

8. Meanwhile, prepare the drizzle. Add the apple cider and brown sugar to a small saucepan. Bring to a simmer over medium heat and cook until reduced by half, about 10 to 15 minutes. Remove from the heat.

9. Carefully place the cake back into the bundt pan. Poke lots of holes all over the cake with a toothpick or cake tester.

10. Slowly drizzle the apple cider mixture over the cake and let sit for at least 30 minutes, or until all of the liquid is absorbed.

11. Store leftovers in an airtight container at room temperature for up to 2 days or in the fridge for up to 4 days.

Vegan option | 8 quart: Make as written

Pineapple Rum Cake

Serves 8

Prep Time: 20 minutes | **Cook Time:** 48 minutes | **Total Time:** 1 hour, 40 minutes

Take a tropical vacation in the form of a bundt cake. Make sure you drain your crushed pineapple well, pressing it through a sieve and reserving the juice for the sauce. There's rum and pineapple in the sauce, too, which soaks into the cake to make it moist and flavorful.

Cake:

2 cups all-purpose flour

1½ teaspoons baking powder

1 teaspoon baking soda

½ teaspoon salt

1 stick unsalted butter (½ cup), softened

½ cup granulated sugar

⅓ cup brown sugar, packed

2 eggs, beaten

1½ teaspoons vanilla extract

⅓ cup dark spiced rum

1 (20-ounce) can crushed pineapple, well-drained and juice reserved

Sauce:

⅓ cup granulated sugar

3 tablespoons dark spiced rum

⅓ cup reserved pineapple juice

1. Add the steam rack to the pot and 1¼ cups water. Grease a 6-cup bundt pan. If needed, create a sling (see page xv)

2. To make the cake, combine the flour, baking powder, baking soda, and salt in a small mixing bowl. Mix and set aside.

3. In a medium mixing bowl, beat the butter, granulated sugar, and brown sugar with an electric mixer for 2 minutes, or until creamy and fluffy. Add the eggs and vanilla and beat until creamy. Add the rum and beat just until mixed, scraping down the sides.

4. Add the flour mixture and stir by hand. Add the drained pineapple and stir just until completely combined.

5. Pour the batter into the prepared pan and smooth out to make level. Cover with aluminum foil. Place on the steam rack and secure the lid.

6. Cook at high pressure for 48 minutes and use a natural release for 30 minutes followed by a quick release.

7. Carefully remove the pan from the pot and remove the foil. The cake should be cooked through. Let cool for a few minutes in the pan before turning out and cooling on a rack while you make the sauce.

8. To make the sauce, combine the sugar and rum in a small saucepan over medium heat. Stir until the sugar has dissolved and bring to a boil. Stop stirring and let the mixture boil for about 3 minutes, or until it turns an amber color. Watch it closely, since it can easily burn.

9. Turn the heat down to low and carefully add the pineapple juice. The mixture will bubble vigorously. Stir until all of the caramel bits have melted back into the sauce.

10. Transfer the cake to a plate and use a brush to paint the sauce all over the cake. Cover every inch of the cake and drizzle any extra over the top. Let the cake sit for at least 30 minutes to soak up the sauce before serving.

11. Store leftovers in an airtight container at room temperature for up to 2 days or in the fridge for up to 4 days.

8 quart: Make as written

Sticky Date Cake

Serves 8

Prep Time: 40 minutes | **Cook Time:** 35 minutes | **Total Time:** 1 hour, 45 minutes

Somewhere between a date cake and sticky toffee pudding, this cake is just right. Homemade date paste gives this cake moisture and natural sweetness, and a caramel sauce on top takes it over the top. The cake is so tender and delicious, though, the sauce isn't required.

Cake:

8 ounces pitted, chopped dates (about 1½ cups)
¾ cup boiling water
½ teaspoon baking soda
1½ cups all-purpose flour
2 teaspoons baking powder
½ teaspoon salt
½ teaspoon ground cinnamon
½ teaspoon ground ginger
¼ teaspoon ground cardamom
1 stick unsalted butter (½ cup), softened
¾ cup granulated sugar
2 eggs, beaten
1 teaspoon vanilla extract

Sauce:

6 tablespoons unsalted butter
¾ cup dark brown sugar, packed
⅓ cup heavy cream
1 tablespoon dark rum (optional)
¼ teaspoon salt

1. Add the steam rack to the pot and 1¼ cups water. Grease a 6-cup bundt pan well, making sure to get in all of the nooks and crannies. If needed, create a sling (see page xv).

2. To make the cake, combine the dates, boiling water, and baking soda in a bowl. Let soak and cool for 15 minutes. Pureé in a blender or small food processor or mash really well to form a smooth paste.

3. In a small mixing bowl, combine the flour, baking powder, salt, cinnamon, ginger, and cardamom. Mix and set aside.

4. In a medium mixing bowl, beat the butter and sugar with an electric mixer for 2 minutes, or until creamy and fluffy. Add the eggs and vanilla and beat until creamy, scraping down the sides.

5. Add the flour mixture and stir by hand until combined. Add the date paste and mix gently just until combined.

6. Pour the batter into the prepared pan and tap on the counter to make level. Cover with aluminum foil. Place on the steam rack and secure the lid.

7. Cook at high pressure for 35 minutes and use a natural release.

8. Carefully remove the pan from the pot and remove the foil. The cake should be cooked through. Let cool for about 15 minutes in the pan before turning out onto a rack. Stick a butter knife in between the pan and the cake in several spots if needed to help the cake separate from the pan.

Recipe continued on page 9

9. Meanwhile, make the sauce. In the pot (cleaned and dried with no steam rack) or a saucepan, add the butter and brown sugar. Using the sauté function or medium heat, melt the butter and sugar together. Add the cream, rum, and salt and stir. Bring to a simmer and cook for 5 to 8 minutes, stirring occasionally, until slightly thickened. It should coat a spoon.

10. Brush half of the sauce over the warm cake. Let the cake cool for at least another 15 minutes and serve warm or at room temperature with more sauce on top. If needed, gently reheat the sauce in the microwave or on the stovetop.

11. Store leftovers in an airtight container at room temperature for up to 3 days. Store the sauce separately.

8 quart: Make as written

NOTES

Dark Chocolate Peppermint Cheesecake

Serves 6

Prep Time: 10 minutes | **Cook Time:** 35 minutes | **Total Time:** 1 hour, 15 minutes, plus chill time

Rich and refreshing—two words that normally don't go together. With a chocolate crust, decadent peppermint cream cheese filling, and dark chocolate shards, this cheesecake is the perfect way to end a meal.

---

1 cup chocolate cookie crumbs (about 4.3 ounces)

4 tablespoons unsalted butter, melted

$^2/_3$ cup plus 2 tablespoons granulated sugar, divided

½ teaspoon salt, divided

2 (8-ounce) packages cream cheese (1 pound), softened

½ cup sour cream

1 tablespoon cornstarch

1 teaspoon vanilla extract

2 teaspoons peppermint extract

2 eggs, room temperature

1 egg yolk, room temperature

2 ounces dark chocolate, finely chopped (or mini chocolate chips)

Chocolate sauce, for decorating

Crushed peppermint candies, for decorating

1. Add the steam rack to the pot and 1¼ cups water. Line the bottom of a 7-inch cheesecake pan with a circle of parchment, leaving the sides of the pan bare. If needed, create a sling (see page xv).

2. In a medium bowl, combine the cookie crumbs, melted butter, 2 tablespoons sugar, and ¼ teaspoon salt. Mix well.

3. Press the cookie crumb mixture into the bottom of the pan, creating a well-packed and even layer. Place in the freezer while you make the filling.

4. In a large bowl, beat the cream cheese and remaining $^2/_3$ cup sugar on medium speed with an electric mixer for a few minutes, or until well mixed and creamy. Add the sour cream, cornstarch, vanilla, peppermint extract, and remaining ¼ teaspoon salt. Beat for another minute.

5. Add the eggs and yolk one at a time, beating after each and scraping down the sides. Fold in the chopped chocolate by hand.

6. Pour the mixture into the prepared cheesecake pan. Tap on the counter several times to dislodge bubbles and use a fork to scrape the top and remove any trapped bubbles.

7. Place the pan, uncovered, on the steam rack and secure the lid.

8. Cook at high pressure for 35 minutes and use a natural release. Carefully remove the lid, taking care not to drip condensation on the cheesecake. The cake should be wiggly but not liquidy.

Recipe continued on page 12

9. Remove the pan and steam rack and let cool on the rack, uncovered, for at least 1 hour. Let cool in the fridge overnight, uncovered.

10. Run a knife around the edge of the cheesecake and remove from the pan by pushing up the bottom and removing the sides of the pan.

11. Serve topped with a drizzle of chocolate sauce and a sprinkle of crushed peppermint.

12. Store leftovers in the fridge in an airtight container for up to 3 days.

Notes:
- Gluten-free cookie crumbs may be substituted.
- Make it a black and white cheesecake by replacing the peppermint extract with another teaspoon of vanilla extract (for a total of 2 teaspoons vanilla).

Gluten-free option | 8 quart: Make as written

NOTES

Mango Cheesecake

Serves 6

Prep Time: 15 minutes | **Cook Time:** 27 minutes | **Total Time:** 1 hour, 10 minutes, plus chill time

Mango purée adds a fruity flavor and airy lightness to this cheesecake. It's not as rich or dense as other cheesecakes, making it a nice warm weather dessert.

1 cup graham cracker crumbs (about 4 ounces)

4 tablespoons unsalted butter, melted

2 tablespoons brown sugar, packed

½ teaspoon salt, divided

2 (8-ounce) packages cream cheese (1 pound), softened

¾ cup granulated sugar

1 tablespoon cornstarch

1 lime, zested and juiced

1 teaspoon vanilla extract

1 cup mango purée

3 eggs, room temperature

1 large ripe mango

1. Add the steam rack to the pot and 1¼ cups water. Line the bottom of a 7-inch cheesecake pan with a circle of parchment, leaving the sides of the pan bare. If needed, create a sling (see page xv).

2. In a medium bowl, combine the graham cracker crumbs, melted butter, brown sugar, and ¼ teaspoon salt. Mix well.

3. Press the graham cracker mixture into the bottom of the pan, creating a well-packed and even layer. Place in the freezer while you make the filling.

4. In a large bowl, beat the cream cheese and sugar with an electric mixer on medium speed for a few minutes, or until well mixed and creamy. Add the cornstarch, lime zest, 2 teaspoons lime juice (reserving the remaining juice), vanilla, and remaining ¼ teaspoon salt. Beat for another minute.

5. Add the mango purée and beat until incorporated. Add the eggs one at a time, beating after each addition and scraping down the sides.

6. Pour the mixture into the prepared cheesecake pan. Tap on the counter several times to dislodge bubbles and use a fork to scrape the top and remove any trapped bubbles.

7. Place the pan, uncovered, on the steam rack and secure the lid.

8. Cook at high pressure for 27 minutes and use a natural release. Carefully remove the lid, taking care not to drip condensation on the cheesecake. The cake should be puffed and wiggly but not liquidy.

Recipe continued on page 14

9. Remove the pan and steam rack and let cool on the rack, uncovered, for at least 1 hour. Let cool in the fridge overnight uncovered.

10. Before serving, peel and cube the ripe mango. Toss with remaining lime juice.

11. Run a knife around the edge of the cheesecake and remove from the pan by pushing up the bottom and removing the sides of the pan.

12. Serve topped with the fresh mango. Store leftovers in the fridge in an airtight container for up to 3 days.

Notes:
- Gluten-free cookie crumbs may be substituted.
- There are a few options for mango purée. In order of preference: canned mango purée (often available in Indian markets), canned diced or whole mango (well drained and puréed), frozen mango (defrosted, drained, and puréed), or fresh mango (puréed). Believe it or not, fresh mango purée offers the least potent flavor to the finished cheesecake.

Gluten-free option | 8 quart: Make as written

NOTES

Salted Peanut Butter Cheesecake

Serves 6

Prep Time: 10 minutes | **Cook Time:** 35 minutes | **Total Time:** 1 hour, 15 minutes, plus chill time

For peanut butter lovers, it doesn't get any better than this. Rich, creamy, and peanut buttery, this cheesecake is the perfect balance of sweet and salty. For a chocolate and peanut butter version, replace the crumbs with chocolate cookies and top with chocolate sauce.

Cheesecake:

1 cup peanut butter cookie crumbs or graham cracker crumbs (about 4 ounces)

4 tablespoons unsalted butter, melted

2/3 cup plus 1 tablespoon granulated sugar, divided

½ teaspoon salt, divided

2 (8-ounce) packages cream cheese (1 pound), softened

½ cup creamy salted peanut butter, room temperature

¼ cup sour cream

1 tablespoon cornstarch

1 teaspoon vanilla extract

1 egg, room temperature

1 egg yolk, room temperature

Topping:

1/3 cup sour cream

¼ cup creamy salted peanut butter, room temperature

3 tablespoons powdered sugar

2 tablespoons chopped roasted, salted peanuts

2 pinches flaky sea salt (optional)

1. Add the steam rack to the pot and 1¼ cups water. Line the bottom of a 7-inch cheesecake pan with a circle of parchment, leaving the sides of the pan bare. If needed, create a sling (see page xv).

2. To make the cheesecake, combine the cookie crumbs, melted butter, 1 tablespoon sugar, and ¼ teaspoon salt in a medium mixing bowl. Mix well.

3. Press the cookie crumb mixture into the bottom of the pan, creating a well-packed and even layer. Place in the freezer while you make the filling.

4. In a large bowl, beat the cream cheese and remaining 2/3 cup sugar with an electric mixer on medium speed for a few minutes, or until well mixed and creamy. Add the peanut butter, sour cream, cornstarch, vanilla, and remaining ¼ teaspoon salt. Beat for another minute.

5. Add the egg and egg yolk one at a time, beating after each addition and scraping down the sides.

6. Pour the mixture into the prepared cheesecake pan and smooth it out so it's level.

7. Place the pan, uncovered, on the steam rack and secure the lid.

8. Cook at high pressure for 35 minutes and use a natural release. Carefully remove the lid, taking care not to drip condensation on the cheesecake. The cake should be wiggly but not liquidy.

9. Remove the pan and steam rack and let cool on the rack, uncovered, for at least 1 hour. Let cool in the fridge overnight, uncovered.

Notes:

- Gluten-free cookie crumbs may be substituted.

10. When ready to serve, prepare the topping. Combine the sour cream, peanut butter, and powdered sugar in a small mixing bowl. Beat until creamy and well mixed.

11. Run a knife around the edge of the cheesecake and remove from the pan by pushing up the bottom and removing the sides of the pan. Top with the sour cream topping and sprinkle with chopped peanuts and sea salt (if using).

Gluten-free option | 8 quart: Make as written

NOTES

Strawberries and Cream Cheesecake

Serves 6

Prep Time: 15 minutes | **Cook Time:** 27 minutes | **Total Time:** 1 hour, 10 minutes, plus chill time

Not only is this cheesecake topped with fresh strawberries and cream, but puréed strawberries are also added to the batter. It's just rich enough to satisfy cheesecake fans and just light enough to win over cheesecake haters.

---

1 cup graham cracker crumbs (about 4 ounces)

4 tablespoons unsalted butter, melted

2 tablespoons brown sugar, packed

½ teaspoon salt, divided

1 pound fresh strawberries, divided

1 tablespoon lemon juice

2 (8-ounce) packages cream cheese (1 pound), softened

¾ cup granulated sugar

1 tablespoon cornstarch

1 teaspoon vanilla extract

2 eggs, room temperature

Up to 1 cup sweetened whipped cream

Up to ¼ cup sour cream (optional)

1. Add the steam rack to the pot and 1¼ cups water. Line the bottom of a 7-inch cheesecake pan with a circle of parchment, leaving the sides of the pan bare. If needed, create a sling (see page xv).

2. In a medium bowl, combine the graham cracker crumbs, melted butter, brown sugar, and ¼ teaspoon salt. Mix well.

3. Press the graham cracker mixture into the bottom of the pan, creating a well-packed and even layer. Place in the freezer while you make the filling.

4. Cap and slice ⅓ of the strawberries. Add to a blender along with the lemon juice. Purée and set aside. Reserve remaining strawberries for garnish.

5. In a large bowl, beat the cream cheese and sugar with an electric mixer on medium speed for a few minutes, or until well mixed and creamy. Add the cornstarch, vanilla, and remaining ¼ teaspoon salt. Beat for another minute.

6. Add ½ cup of the strawberry purée and beat until incorporated. Reserve any remaining purée for garnish. Add the eggs one at a time, beating after each addition and scraping down the sides.

7. Pour the mixture into the prepared cheesecake pan. Tap on the counter several times to dislodge bubbles and use a fork to scrape the top and remove any trapped bubbles.

8. Place the pan, uncovered, on the steam rack and secure the lid.

9. Cook at high pressure for 27 minutes and use a natural release. Carefully remove the lid, taking care not to drip condensation on the cheesecake. The cake should be puffed and wiggly but not liquidy.

Recipe continued on 20

Notes:

- Gluten-free cookie crumbs may be substituted.
- If you like your cheesecake tart, replace up to ¼ cup of the whipped cream topping with sour cream. Adjust the mixture according to your tastes. If you want to keep your cheesecake light, don't add any sour cream and just use 1 cup of whipped cream.

10. Remove the pan and steam rack and let cool on the rack, uncovered, for at least 1 hour. Let cool in the fridge overnight, uncovered.

11. Run a knife around the edge of the cheesecake and remove from the pan by pushing up the bottom and removing the sides of the pan.

12. Mix the whipped cream and sour cream (if using, see note). Spread on top. Cap the remaining strawberries and dice. Toss with any remaining purée and arrange on top of the whipped cream mixture. Serve immediately.

13. Store leftovers in the fridge in an airtight container for up to 3 days.

Gluten-free option | 8 quart: Make as written

NOTES

Classic Carrot Cake

Serves 6

Prep Time: 15 minutes | **Cook Time:** 55 minutes | **Total Time:** 1 hour, 40 minutes

Carrot cake is a classic for a reason. Extra moist with creamy icing, this cake is sure to enter your regular rotation.

Cake:

½ cup neutral oil (canola, grapeseed, or vegetable)

⅓ cup granulated sugar

⅓ cup brown sugar, packed

2 eggs, beaten

1½ teaspoons baking powder

¾ teaspoon ground cinnamon

¼ teaspoon ground ginger

⅛ teaspoon ground cloves

¼ teaspoon salt

½ teaspoon vanilla extract

1 cup all-purpose flour

1¼ cups grated carrots

¼ cup raisins (optional)

¼ cup chopped pecans or walnuts (optional, plus more for decoration)

Frosting:

4 ounces cream cheese, softened

4 tablespoons unsalted butter, softened

1½ cups powdered sugar

¼ teaspoon orange or lemon zest

¼ teaspoon vanilla extract

1 pinch salt

1. Add the steam rack to the pot and 1¼ cups water. Grease a 7-inch baking pan. Optional: line the bottom with a circle of parchment first. If needed, create a sling (see page xv).

2. To make the cake, add the oil, granulated sugar, brown sugar, eggs, baking powder, cinnamon, ginger, cloves, salt, and vanilla to a medium mixing bowl. Beat with an electric mixer until well mixed. Add the flour and beat just until mixed.

3. Add the carrots, raisins, and nuts (if using), and mix by hand just until combined. Pour into the prepared baking pan and tap on the counter a few times to level out the mixture.

4. Cover the pan with aluminum foil. Place on the steam rack and secure the lid.

5. Cook at high pressure for 55 minutes and use a natural release for 15 minutes followed by a quick release.

6. Carefully remove the pan from the pot and remove the foil. The cake should be puffed up but firm to the touch. Let cool for a few minutes before removing the cake from the pan and placing it on a cooling rack. Let cool completely.

7. To make the frosting, combine the cream cheese and butter in a small mixing bowl. Beat with an electric mixer until very smooth and creamy, scraping down the sides of the bowl. Add the powdered sugar ½ cup at a time, beating after each addition. Add the zest, vanilla, and salt, and beat until fully mixed and creamy.

8. Frost the top and sides of the cooled cake and decorate with chopped or whole nuts (optional). Store leftovers in the fridge in an airtight container for up to 3 days.

Recipe continued on page 23

Note:
- Make it gluten-free by replacing the flour with your favorite gluten-free all-purpose flour mix.
- Make it vegan by replacing the eggs with egg replacer (follow package directions). Make the frosting with vegan cream cheese and vegan butter or omit altogether and top with a dusting of powdered sugar.

Gluten-free option | Vegan option
8 quart: Make as written

NOTES

Chocolate-Orange Lava Cakes

Serves 4

Prep Time: 10 minutes | **Cook Time:** 9 minutes | **Total Time:** 30 minutes

For the ultimate in decadent chocolate desserts, only a lava cake will do. Based on Melissa Clark's recipe, this version adds a hint of orange using zest and extract. What kind of chocolate you use depends on how intense you want this dessert to be—use a mix of bittersweet and semisweet for a nice balance.

---

1 stick unsalted butter (½ cup)

6 ounces semisweet or bittersweet chocolate, chopped (or chocolate chips)

1 cup powdered sugar

¼ teaspoon salt

3 eggs

1 egg yolk

1 teaspoon finely grated orange zest

1 teaspoon orange extract

1 teaspoon vanilla extract

¼ cup plus 2 tablespoons all-purpose flour

1. Add the steam rack to the pot and 1¼ cups water. Butter four 6 or 7-ounce ramekins.

2. Melt the butter and chocolate together. Using a microwave: heat in 30-second increments in a heatproof bowl, stirring between each increment. On the stovetop: add to a small saucepan and heat, stirring, over medium-low heat just until melted.

3. Add the melted butter and chocolate to a medium mixing bowl. Add the powdered sugar and salt and whisk until mixed. Add the eggs, egg yolk, orange zest, orange extract, and vanilla and whisk. Add the flour and whisk just until combined.

4. Add an equal amount of batter to each prepared ramekin. Cover each with aluminum foil and place on the steam rack. Secure the lid.

5. Cook at high pressure for 9 minutes and use a quick release.

6. Carefully remove from the cooker and let sit for 3 minutes, still covered. Remove the foil and run a knife around the edge between the cake and the ramekin. Invert onto a plate and serve immediately.

3 quart: Cook in batches | 8 quart: Make as written

Dried Cherry and Pecan Fruit Cake

Serves 10

Prep Time: 45 minutes | **Cook Time:** 70 minutes | **Total Time:** 2 hours, 30 minutes

Fruit cake gets a bad rap, but a good one is *the* holiday dessert. Studded with liqueur-soaked dried cherries, crystallized ginger, and pecans, you'll be pulling this recipe out year after year. Don't let the 7-inch diameter fool you—this cake is tall and dense and can easily feed ten.

1 cup dried cherries

1 cup raisins

$2/3$ cup pitted, chopped dates

$1/3$ cup chopped crystallized
　　ginger

½ cup amaretto or hazelnut
　　liqueur

½ cup whiskey or rum

1½ cups all-purpose flour

1½ teaspoons baking powder

½ teaspoon salt

½ teaspoon ground cinnamon

1 pinch ground nutmeg

1 stick unsalted butter (½ cup),
　　softened

1 cup dark brown sugar, packed

2 eggs, room temperature

2 tablespoons molasses or
　　dark golden syrup

½ teaspoon finely grated
　　lemon or orange zest

1 cup chopped pecans

1. Combine the dried cherries, raisins, chopped dates, crystalized ginger, liqueur, and whiskey or rum in the pot. Turn on the sauté function and bring to a boil. Boil 1 minute and turn off the sauté function. Pour the fruit and liquid into a bowl. Let the fruit soak and cool for at least 30 minutes. Clean out the pot.

2. Add the steam rack to the pot and 1¼ cups water. Grease a 7-inch baking pan. Optional: line the bottom with a circle of parchment first. If needed, create a sling (see page xv).

3. In a small mixing bowl, combine the flour, baking powder, salt, cinnamon, and nutmeg. Mix and set aside.

4. In a medium mixing bowl, beat the butter and brown sugar with an electric mixer for 2 minutes, or until creamy and fluffy. Add the eggs, molasses, and zest and beat until creamy. Add the flour mixture and beat just until combined.

5. Add the dried fruit, any soaking liquid, and the pecans, and stir by hand just until mixed.

6. Pour the batter into the prepared pan and smooth out to make level. Cover with aluminum foil. Place on the steam rack and secure the lid.

7. Cook at high pressure for 70 minutes and use a natural release.

8. Remove the pan and steam rack and remove the foil. The cake should be puffed up but firm to the touch. Let cool completely in the pan before serving.

9. Store leftovers in an airtight container at room temperature for up to 5 days.

Note:
- Make it gluten-free by replacing the flour with your favorite gluten-free all-purpose flour mix.
- Make this recipe your own by swapping out the dried fruit, nuts, and alcohol for your favorites. Dried apricots and pineapple work well, walnuts can be switched for pecans, or replace all or part of the booze with brandy.
- If desired, the alcohol can be swapped for fruit juice like apple or pineapple.

Gluten-free option | 8 quart: Make as written

NOTES

Flourless Chocolate Cake

Serves 6–8

Prep Time: 10 minutes | **Cook Time:** 35 minutes | **Total Time:** 1 hour, 10 minutes

Dense, rich, and oh-so-chocolatey, this cake will satisfy even the most serious chocolate lovers. Make it even richer by finishing with a dusting of cocoa powder, or lighten it up a bit with a sprinkle of powdered sugar or dollop of whipped cream.

4 ounces bittersweet, semisweet, or dark chocolate (chopped or chocolate chips)

1 stick unsalted butter (½ cup)

¾ cup granulated sugar

½ cup unsweetened cocoa powder

1 teaspoon espresso powder (optional)

1 teaspoon vanilla extract

½ teaspoon salt

4 large eggs

Powdered sugar or cocoa powder, for serving (optional)

1. Add the steam rack to the pot and 1¼ cups water. Grease a 7-inch baking pan. If needed, create a sling (see page xv).

2. In a medium heatproof bowl, melt the chocolate and butter in the microwave in short bursts, or melt over a double boiler. Whisk to combine. Add the sugar, cocoa powder, espresso powder (if using), vanilla, and salt. Whisk well until totally combined.

3. Add the eggs to a large bowl. Beat for about 5 minutes with an electric mixer, or until the eggs are frothy and have doubled in size.

4. Stir the chocolate mixture again and fold it to the eggs a little at a time just until mixed. The mixture should be uniform but airy.

5. Pour into the prepared pan and cover with aluminum foil. Place on the steam rack and secure the lid.

6. Cook at high pressure for 35 minutes and use a natural release.

7. Remove the pan and steam rack and remove the foil. The cake should be dense and solid, not jiggly. Let cool completely on the rack.

8. Serve topped with a dusting of powdered sugar or cocoa powder. Store leftovers in an airtight container at room temperature for up to 3 days.

Gluten-free | 8 quart: Make as written

Plum Cornmeal Cake

Serves 6

Prep Time: 10 minutes | **Cook Time:** 45 minutes | **Total Time:** 1 hour, 20 minutes

This take on an Italian polenta cake swaps the coarser ground corn for fine cornmeal and cooks up moist and tender in the pressure cooker. If you don't have dark plums, swap for fresh apricots or nectarines.

¾ cup all-purpose flour

½ cup finely-ground cornmeal

2 teaspoons baking powder

¼ teaspoon ground cardamom
or ½ teaspoon ground
cinnamon

¼ teaspoon salt

1 pinch ground nutmeg

1 stick unsalted butter (½ cup),
softened

²/₃ cup granulated sugar

2 eggs plus 1 egg yolk

½ teaspoon finely grated
lemon or lime zest

½ teaspoon vanilla extract

¼ teaspoon almond extract
(optional)

2 tablespoons milk

2 medium dark plums, pitted
and cut into quarters

1 tablespoon brown sugar,
packed

1. Add the steam rack to the pot and 1¼ cups water. Grease a 7-inch baking or cheesecake pan. Optional: line the bottom with a circle of parchment first. If needed, create a sling (see page xv).

2. In a small mixing bowl, combine the flour, cornmeal, baking powder, cardamom or cinnamon, salt, and nutmeg. Mix and set aside.

3. In a medium mixing bowl, beat the butter and granulated sugar with an electric mixer for 2 minutes, or until creamy and fluffy. Add the eggs and egg yolk one at a time, beating after each addition. Add the zest, vanilla, and almond extract (if using) and beat until mixed, scraping down the sides.

4. Add half of the flour mixture and beat. Add the rest of the flour and the milk and beat until completely combined.

5. Pour the batter into the prepared pan and smooth out to make level. Add the plums in a single layer, skin-side up. Sprinkle with the brown sugar. Cover with aluminum foil. Place on the steam rack and secure the lid.

6. Cook at high pressure for 45 minutes and use a natural release.

7. Carefully remove the pan from the pot and remove the foil. The cake should be puffed and cooked through. Let cool completely on a rack before serving.

8. Store leftovers in an airtight container at room temperature for up to 2 days.

8 quart: Make as written

Pineapple Upside Down Cake

Serves 6

Prep Time: 10 minutes | **Cook Time:** 40 minutes | **Total Time:** 1 hour, 20 minutes

A classic cake, pineapple upside-down cake is a tasty combination of moist cake, caramel sauce, and tender fruit. Don't forget to line the bottom with parchment and grease the pan; it'll make flipping the cake over much easier.

Topping:

4 tablespoons unsalted butter, melted

1/3 cup brown sugar, packed

4 pineapple rings in juice, drained

5 maraschino cherries, drained

Cake:

1 stick unsalted butter (½ cup), softened

½ cup brown sugar, packed

2 eggs

1 teaspoon vanilla extract

1¼ cups all-purpose flour, divided

2 teaspoons baking powder

¼ teaspoon ground cinnamon

¼ teaspoon salt

¼ cup buttermilk or whole milk

1. Add the steam rack to the pot and 1¼ cups water. Line the bottom of a 7-inch baking pan with a circle of parchment and grease the whole pan. If needed, create a sling (see page xv).

2. To make the topping, whisk together the melted butter and brown sugar in a small mixing bowl. Pour into the prepared pan. Add the pineapple rings on top in a single layer. Four rings should fit snugly in a 7-inch pan. Place the cherries inside each of the rings and one in the center of the cake.

3. To make the cake, beat the butter and brown sugar with an electric mixer for 2 minutes in a medium mixing bowl, or until fluffy. Add the eggs and vanilla and beat until creamy. Scrape down the sides.

4. Add half of the flour along with the baking powder, cinnamon, and salt and beat. Add the buttermilk and beat. Add the rest of the flour and beat just until completely combined.

5. Pour the batter on top of the pineapple and smooth out to make level, careful not to disturb the pineapple and sealing the cake over the sauce. Cover with aluminum foil. Place on the steam rack and secure the lid.

6. Cook at high pressure for 40 minutes and use a natural release.

7. Carefully remove the pan from the pot and remove the foil. The cake should be cooked through. Let cool for 3 minutes. Cover the pan with a serving plate, grab the back of the pan (it will be hot—use oven mitts), and flip over.

Recipe continued on page 34

8. Remove the pan and peel off the parchment and let the cake cool for at least 15 minutes. Serve warm or at room temperature.

9. Store leftovers in an airtight container at room temperature for up to 2 days.

8 quart: Make as written

NOTES

Lemon-Ricotta Mini Cakes

Serves 4

Prep Time: 10 minutes | **Cook Time:** 30 minutes | **Total Time:** 1 hour

More of a British-style pudding than a cake, these tender little desserts are lightly sweet, lightly tart, and ultra lemony. Serve them warm with the runny sauce and a dollop of whipped cream.

½ cup sugar, plus more for dusting ramekins

¼ cup all-purpose flour

¼ teaspoon salt

2 eggs, separated

⅓ cup ricotta cheese

⅓ cup milk

5 tablespoons fresh lemon juice, divided

½ teaspoon finely grated lemon zest

¼ cup plus 2 tablespoons powdered sugar

Note:
- Make it gluten-free by replacing the flour with your favorite gluten-free all-purpose flour mix.

1. Add the steam rack to the pot and 1¼ cups water. Butter and sugar four 6- or 7-ounce ramekins.

2. In a small mixing bowl, sift together the sugar, flour, and salt. Set aside.

3. In another small mixing bowl, beat the egg whites with an electric mixer until soft peaks form. Set aside.

4. In a medium mixing bowl, beat together the egg yolks, ricotta cheese, milk, 3 tablespoons lemon juice, and zest. Add the flour mixture slowly while beating just until mixed. Carefully fold in the egg whites by hand, careful not to overmix.

5. Add an equal amount of batter to each prepared ramekin. Cover each with aluminum foil and place on the steam rack. Secure the lid.

6. Cook at low pressure for 30 minutes and use a natural release for 10 minutes followed by a quick release.

7. Meanwhile, make the sauce. In a small bowl, whisk the remaining 2 tablespoons of lemon juice and the powdered sugar until mixed.

8. Carefully remove the ramekins from the cooker and remove the foil. Invert onto a plate and top with sauce. Serve warm.

Gluten-free option
3 quart: Cook in batches | 8 quart: Make as written

Fruit Desserts

Cobblers, Crumbles, and Dumplings
Individual Rhubarb Cobblers 39
Mini Blueberry and Almond Crisps 41
Mixed Berry Cobbler 42
Stone Fruit Crumble 43
Peach Dumplings 45

Poached Fruit
"Baked" Apples 47
Spiced Poached Pears 48

Individual Rhubarb Cobblers

Serves 3

Prep Time: 10 minutes | **Cook Time:** 18 minutes | **Total Time:** 45 minutes

Rhubarb is crazy tart when left to its own devices, but coated in sugar and paired with a cakey base, it becomes a delightfully sweet-tart cobbler. You can swap pitted sour cherries for the rhubarb if you like.

Fruit topping:

1½ cups rhubarb, diced (about 3 large or 6 small stalks)

¼ cup granulated sugar

2 teaspoons cornstarch

½ teaspoon vanilla extract

Cake:

²/₃ cup all-purpose flour

¼ cup granulated sugar

1¼ teaspoons baking powder

1 pinch salt

3 tablespoons unsalted butter, melted

3 tablespoons milk

½ teaspoon vanilla extract

Note:

- Make it vegan by replacing the butter with vegan margarine and the milk with nondairy milk.

1. Add the steam rack to the pot and 1¼ cups water. Butter three 6- or 7-ounce ramekins or half-pint mason jars.

2. To make the fruit topping, combine the rhubarb, sugar, cornstarch, and vanilla in a bowl and mix. Set aside.

3. To make the cake, combine the flour, sugar, baking powder, and salt in a small mixing bowl. Mix. Add the melted butter, milk, and vanilla and stir just until combined.

4. Add an equal amount of cake batter to each ramekin or jar. Toss the rhubarb and add an equal amount on top of each including any syrup.

5. Cover each with aluminum foil and place on the steam rack. Secure the lid.

6. Cook at high pressure for 18 minutes and use a natural release.

7. Carefully remove from the cooker and remove the foil. Let cool on the counter for several minutes before serving. The cake should be cooked through and the rhubarb should be gooey.

8. Serve warm with a dollop of whipped cream or vanilla ice cream.

Vegan option
3 quart: Cook in batches | 8 quart: Make as written

Mini Blueberry and Almond Crisps

Serves 2–4

Prep Time: 10 minutes | **Cook Time:** 7 minutes | **Total Time:** 30 minutes

Fruity and buttery, this versatile dessert can be made vegan or gluten-free and is good for breakfast, too. Swap the blueberries for blackberries if that's what you have on hand.

Fruit filling:

1½ cups frozen or fresh
blueberries

1 tablespoon granulated sugar

1 tablespoon cornstarch

2 teaspoons fresh lemon juice

¼ teaspoon finely grated
lemon zest

Topping:

¼ cup almond flour

¼ cup rolled oats

¼ cup brown sugar, packed

1 pinch salt

1 pinch ground nutmeg

2 tablespoons unsalted butter,
cubed

1 heaping tablespoon slivered
or chopped almonds

Notes:
- Make it vegan by replacing the butter with coconut oil or vegan margarine.
- Make it with no added sugar by using a sugar substitute. Follow the sugar replacement instructions on the box.

1. Add the steam rack to the pot and 1¼ cups water. Grease two 7- or 8-ounce ramekins or three 5- or 6-ounce ramekins.

2. To make the fruit filling, combine the blueberries, sugar, cornstarch, lemon juice, and zest in a small mixing bowl. Divide mixture evenly between the ramekins.

3. To make the topping, combine the almond flour, rolled oats, brown sugar, salt, and nutmeg in another small mixing bowl. Mix. Add the butter and use a pastry blender or your fingers to press the butter and flour mixture together, working until moistened and no pieces of butter are bigger than a pea. Add the almonds and toss.

4. Sprinkle the mixture evenly over both ramekins. Place the ramekins on the steam rack and secure the lid.

5. Cook at high pressure for 7 minutes and use a natural release.

6. Carefully remove the lid, taking care not to drip condensation on the crisps. Let cool for a few minutes before serving.

7. If desired, place under the broiler for a few minutes to crisp up. Be careful not to let the crisps burn.

8. Serve warm with a dollop of whipped cream or vanilla ice cream.

Gluten-free | Vegan option | No-added-sugar option
3 quart: Make as written | 8 quart: Make as written

Mixed Berry Cobbler

Serves 5–6

Prep Time: 10 minutes | **Cook Time:** 30 minutes | **Total Time:** 1 hour, 10 minutes

While you technically can make cobbler right in the pot, you risk either getting a "burn" warning on your Instant Pot or liquidy fruit. Cooking the cobbler pot-in-pot and toasting under a broiler for a few minutes yields beautiful results.

Fruit filling:

3 cups mixed berries (fresh, frozen, or a mix of the two)

2 tablespoons granulated sugar

1½–2 tablespoons cornstarch

1 tablespoon lemon juice

½ teaspoon vanilla extract

Cake topping:

¾ cup all-purpose flour

½ cup granulated sugar, plus extra for sprinkling on top

1½ teaspoons baking powder

¼ teaspoon salt

3 tablespoons unsalted butter, cubed

5 tablespoons milk

Notes:

- Make it a peach cobbler by simply switching the berries for fresh or frozen peaches and cutting the cornstarch in half.
- Make it with no added sugar by using a sugar substitute. Follow the sugar replacement instructions on the box.

1. Add the steam rack to the pot and 1¼ cups water. Grease a 6- or 7-inch baking pan or dish. If needed, create a sling (see page xv).

2. To make the fruit filling, toss together the berries, sugar, cornstarch, lemon juice, and vanilla in a small mixing bowl. If using fresh berries, use 1½ tablespoons cornstarch. If using frozen berries, use 2 tablespoons cornstarch. Pour berry mixture into the prepared baking pan.

3. To make the cake, mix together the flour, sugar, baking powder, and salt in a small mixing bowl. Add the butter and use your hands to squish the butter into the flour mixture, tossing and repeating until the mixture resembles moist cornmeal.

4. Add the milk and mix until combined. Drop large spoonfuls onto the berries in a single layer. Cover with aluminum foil and place on the steam rack. Secure the lid.

5. Cook at high pressure for 30 minutes and use a natural release for 30 minutes followed by a quick release.

6. Carefully remove from the cooker and remove the foil. The topping should be puffed and cooked through. For best results, sprinkle with sugar and place under the broiler for a few minutes to crisp the top. Let cool on the counter for several minutes before serving.

7. Serve warm with a dollop of whipped cream or vanilla ice cream. Store leftovers in the fridge in an airtight container for up to 2 days.

No-added-sugar option
3 quart: Make as written using a 6-inch pan
8 quart: Make as written

Stone Fruit Crumble

Serves 5–6

Prep Time: 10 minutes | **Cook Time:** 10 minutes | **Total Time:** 40 minutes

Stone fruit like peaches, nectarines, plums, and apricots are in season for a few glorious months in the summer. Use any excess bounty to make this fruity crumble and serve with ice cream. Or serve with plain yogurt for a sweet breakfast.

Fruit filling:

1 pound stone fruit (about
    4 cups), pitted, peeled if
    desired, and sliced
¼ cup granulated sugar
3 tablespoons all-purpose flour

Topping:

¾ cup all-purpose flour
1/3 cup brown sugar, packed
¼ teaspoon salt
1 pinch ground nutmeg
6 tablespoons unsalted butter,
    cubed

Notes:

- Make it vegan by replacing the butter with coconut oil or vegan margarine.
- Make it with no added sugar by using a sugar substitute. Follow the sugar replacement instructions on the box.

1. Add the steam rack to the pot and 1¼ cups water. Grease a 6- or 7-inch baking pan or dish. If needed, create a sling (see page xv).

2. To make the fruit filling, combine the fruit, sugar, and flour in the prepared pan. Toss to mix and set aside.

3. To make the topping, combine the flour, brown sugar, salt, and nutmeg in a small mixing bowl. Mix. Add the butter and use a pastry blender or your fingers to press the butter and flour mixture together, working until moistened and no pieces of butter are bigger than a pea.

4. Sprinkle the mixture evenly over the fruit. Cover with aluminum foil and place on the steam rack. Secure the lid.

5. Cook at high pressure for 10 minutes and use a natural release for 10 minutes followed by a quick release.

6. Carefully remove from the cooker and remove the foil. The fruit should be bubbly and the topping cooked. For best results, place under the broiler for a few minutes to crisp the top. Let cool on the counter for several minutes before serving.

7. Serve warm with a dollop of whipped cream or vanilla ice cream.

Vegan option | No-added-sugar option
3 quart: Make as written using a 6-inch pan
8 quart: Make as written

Peach Dumplings

Serves 4

Prep Time: 10 minutes | **Cook Time:** 12 minutes | **Total Time:** 40 minutes

For this recipe, using canned crescent rolls is a shortcut that pays off big time. The rolls, wrapped around slices of peach (frozen will work here), soak up the brown sugar-butter-peach nectar sauce and turn into something magical. Serve warm with the sauce spooned over top and a scoop of vanilla ice cream.

1 (8-ounce) can crescent rolls

1 large peach or 2 small peaches, cut into 8 thick slices

6 tablespoons unsalted butter, melted

1 cup peach nectar or juice

½ cup brown sugar, packed

½ teaspoon ground cinnamon

Vanilla ice cream or whipped cream, for serving

1. Unroll the crescent rolls and divide into triangles. Wrap each peach slice, starting with the widest part of the dough first, and roll up completely.

2. Add the melted butter and peach nectar to the pot. Place the dumplings on top in a single layer. Sprinkle the brown sugar and cinnamon over the top and secure the lid.

3. Cook at high pressure for 12 minutes and use a natural release.

4. The dumplings should be cooked through and the sauce thickened. Let the dumplings cool for 10 minutes before serving.

5. Serve warm, drizzled with sauce from the pot. Top with vanilla ice cream or whipped cream.

6. Store leftovers in the fridge in an airtight container for up to 3 days.

3 quart: Make as written | 8 quart: Make as written or double

"Baked" Apples

Serves 4

Prep Time: 10 minutes | **Cook Time:** 8–10 minutes | **Total Time:** 35 minutes

Cooking the apples whole with just a dollop of cinnamon-sugar butter brings out their appley flavor. Use whatever variety of firm apple you like—just keep in mind the cook time can vary slightly. I've had good luck with Pink Ladies and similar varieties.

5–6 medium apples

5 tablespoons unsalted butter, softened

3 tablespoons brown sugar, packed

½ teaspoon ground cinnamon

2 tablespoons chopped pecans or walnuts (optional)

1 heaping tablespoon raisins (optional)

1 cup apple cider or apple juice

Notes:
- Make it vegan by using vegan butter.
- Make it with no added sugar by using a sugar substitute. Follow the sugar replacement instructions on the box.
- If your cooker doesn't have a low pressure setting, cook at high pressure for 5 minutes instead.

1. Core the apples, leaving the bottom ¼ of the apple solid to keep the butter mixture from leaking out. Scrape out any seeds.

2. In a small bowl, mix the butter, brown sugar, cinnamon, nuts, and raisins (if using). Add equal amounts to the empty core of each apple.

3. Add the apple cider to the pot. Set the apples in the cider upright. Secure the lid.

4. Cook at low pressure for 8 to 10 minutes depending on the size and firmness of your apples. Use a natural release.

5. Check the apples for doneness. If they aren't as tender if you'd like, return them to the pot and cook for another 2 minutes. Note that if they cook for too long then they can completely lose their shape.

6. Serve warm.

Gluten-free | Vegan option | No-added-sugar option
3 quart: Halve the recipe | 8 quart: Make as written

Spiced Poached Pears

Serves 6

Prep Time: 20 minutes | **Cook Time:** 4 minutes | **Total Time:** 1 hour

Ruby red wine-poached pears make an elegant dessert or brunch side dish. Serve warm or cold, drizzled with a little sauce.

---

2 cups red wine

3 cups water

1 cup granulated sugar

1 (1-inch) piece ginger, sliced

2 cinnamon sticks

4 whole cloves

2 slices orange or lemon

6 pears (firm)

Notes:
- White wine can be used instead, but your pears won't be a nice ruby red.
- Make it with no added sugar by using a sugar substitute. Follow the sugar replacement instructions on the box. Alternatively, replace the water with fruit juice and omit the sugar.

1. Add the wine, water, sugar, ginger, cinnamon, cloves, and orange to the pot. Turn on the sauté function and bring to a boil. Simmer for 1 minute and turn off the sauté function.

2. Peel the pears, leaving them whole and leaving the stem attached. Add them to the pot and secure the lid.

3. Cook at high pressure for 2 to 4 minutes and use a natural release for 30 minutes followed by a quick release. The cook time will depend on the size and ripeness of your pears. For large, very unripe pears, cook for 4 minutes. The pears should be whole but easily pierced by a knife.

4. Remove the pears with a slotted spoon and set aside. Remove the spices and orange and discard. Discard about one-third of the cooking liquid. Turn on the sauté function and simmer the remaining liquid for 10 to 15 minutes, or until reduced by about one-third.

5. Serve warm, or store the pears in the liquid and refrigerate for a few hours and serve cold.

Gluten-free | Vegan | No-added-sugar option
3 quart: Reduce the recipe by $1/3$ | 8 quart: Make as written

Puddings, Pies, and Custards

Bread Puddings
Chocolate Rye Bread Pudding 53
Individual Butter Pecan Croissant Bread Puddings 54
Raspberry Challah Bread Pudding 55

Pies
Brownie Pie with Peanut Butter Swirl 59
Ginger Pumpkin Pie 60
Mini Sweet Potato Pies 63

Puddings and Flans
Matcha Crème Brûlée 65
Mini Flans 66
Spiced Chocolate Flan 69
Dark Chocolate Pudding 71
White Chocolate Pots De Crème 73

Rice Puddings
Amaretto-Cherry Rice Pudding 74
Bourbon Cinnamon Raisin Brown Rice Pudding 77
Coconut Sticky Rice with Mango 79
Tiramisu Rice Pudding 80

Chocolate Rye Bread Pudding

Serves 6–8

Prep Time: 25 minutes | **Cook Time:** 30 minutes | **Total Time:** 1 hour, 30 minutes

Rye and chocolate? It's a surprisingly delicious combination. Adjust the chocolate in this recipe to suit your tastes—all dark chocolate for a chocolate lover, a mix of milk and semisweet or even white chocolate and semisweet for a sweet tooth. Marble rye also works great.

½ cup granulated sugar

¼ cup unsweetened cocoa

½ teaspoon salt

3 eggs, beaten

2 cups whole milk

1½ teaspoons vanilla extract

9 ounces stale or oven-dried rye bread, cut into 1-inch cubes (about 5 cups lightly packed)

¾ cup semisweet or dark chocolate chips or chunks

Chocolate sauce, for serving

Notes:

- Stale bread cubes work best for this recipe. If your bread is still soft, pop the cubed pieces into a 300°F oven for 15 minutes. Let cool completely before using.
- If your cooker doesn't have a low pressure setting, cook at high pressure for 20 minutes instead.

1. Add the steam rack to the pot and 1¼ cups water. Grease a 7-inch baking pan. If needed, create a sling (see page xv).

2. In a large mixing bowl, whisk together the sugar, cocoa, and salt until no lumps remain. Add the eggs and whisk. Add the milk and vanilla and whisk.

3. Add the bread and stir to combine. Let sit for 15 to 20 minutes so the bread can soak up some of the liquid.

4. Stir again and add half the mixture to the pan. Top with half the chocolate. Add the remaining bread mixture and sprinkle with the rest of the chocolate. Place, uncovered, on the steam rack and secure the lid.

5. Cook at low pressure for 30 minutes and use a natural release.

6. Carefully remove the lid, taking care not to drip condensation on the bread pudding. It should be a little jiggly but solid.

7. Remove the pan and steam rack and let cool on the rack for at least 20 minutes. Serve warm or at room temperature topped with chocolate sauce.

8. Store leftovers in the fridge in an airtight container for up to 3 days.

> 8 quart: Make as written

Individual Butter Pecan Croissant Bread Puddings

Serves 4

Prep Time: 25 minutes | **Cook Time:** 12 minutes | **Total Time:** 1 hour

Flaky croissants and toasted, buttery pecans make for one tasty bread pudding. This is a perfect way to use up day-old, stale croissants and turn them into a whole new dish.

3 tablespoons unsalted butter

$\frac{1}{3}$ cup chopped pecans

1 egg

1 egg yolk

$\frac{1}{3}$ cup brown sugar, packed

¼ teaspoon salt

$\frac{1}{3}$ cup heavy cream

½ cup whole milk

½ teaspoon vanilla extract

¼ teaspoon butter rum extract (optional)

3 stale or oven-dried croissants, ripped into chunks (about 6 ounces, or 5 cups lightly packed)

Granulated sugar, for sprinkling on top

Notes:
- If your cooker doesn't have a low pressure setting, cook at high pressure for 8 minutes instead.

1. Add the steam rack to the pot and 1¼ cups water. Grease four 6- or 7-ounce ramekins.

2. In a small saucepan, melt the butter over medium heat. Add the pecans and coat with the butter. Cook, swirling the pan occasionally, for about 2 minutes, or until the foaming butter is a light brown and the nuts are toasted. Set aside to cool.

3. In a large mixing bowl, whisk together the egg, egg yolk, brown sugar, and salt until well mixed. Add the heavy cream, milk, vanilla, and butter rum extract (if using) and whisk.

4. Add the croissants and toss to coat completely. Let sit for 15 minutes so the bread can soak up some of the liquid.

5. Stir again and add half of the croissant mixture to each ramekin. Top with half of the pecans and the browned butter. Add the remaining croissant mixture. Reserve the rest of the pecans for garnish. Place, uncovered, on the steam rack and secure the lid.

6. Cook at low pressure for 12 minutes and use a natural release.

7. Carefully remove the lid, taking care not to drip condensation on the bread puddings. They should be puffed and a little jiggly but solid.

8. Carefully remove the ramekins. Sprinkle each with granulated sugar and broil for 2 to 3 minutes, until toasted. Top with remaining pecans and serve warm or at room temperature.

3 quart: Cook in batches | 8 quart: Make as written

Raspberry Challah Bread Pudding

Serves 6–8

Prep Time: 25 minutes | **Cook Time:** 30 minutes | **Total Time:** 1 hour, 15 minutes

Challah is a lightly sweet and eggy bread that should never be wasted. Luckily, it makes fantastic bread pudding. If you have half a loaf lying around, then put it to good use by making this indulgent dessert. Brioche can step in for the challah in a pinch.

Bread Pudding:

1½ cups whole milk

1 cup heavy cream

3 eggs, beaten

²/₃ cup granulated sugar, plus more for sprinkling on top

2 teaspoons vanilla extract

¼ teaspoon salt

9 ounces stale or oven-dried challah bread, cut into 1-inch cubes (about 6 cups lightly packed)

¼ cup chopped white chocolate (or white chocolate chips)

Sauce:

10 ounces fresh or frozen raspberries

¼ cup granulated sugar

1 tablespoon raspberry liqueur or water

2 teaspoons lemon juice

1½ teaspoons cornstarch

1. Add the steam rack to the pot and 1¼ cups water. Grease a 7-inch baking pan. If needed, create a sling (see page xv).

2. To make the bread pudding, whisk together the milk, heavy cream, eggs, ²/₃ cup sugar, vanilla, and salt in a large mixing bowl. Add the bread and stir to combine. Let sit for 10 minutes so the bread can soak up some of the liquid.

3. Add the white chocolate chips and toss the mixture again. Pour into the prepared pan. Place, uncovered, on the steam rack and secure the lid.

4. Cook at low pressure for 30 minutes and use a natural release.

5. Meanwhile, make the sauce. Combine the raspberries and sugar in a small saucepan. Mash the berries and mix with the sugar. Cook over medium-low heat until bubbling.

6. In a small bowl, combine the liqueur or water, lemon juice, and cornstarch and mix until the cornstarch has dissolved. Add to the saucepan and stir. Bring to a simmer and cook for 1 minute.

7. If desired, push through a fine-mesh strainer to remove the seeds. Place the sauce in the refrigerator until ready to serve.

8. Once the pressure has released, carefully remove the lid, taking care not to drip condensation on the bread pudding. It should be a little jiggly but solid.

Recipe continued on page 57

Notes:

- Stale bread cubes work best for this recipe. If your bread is still soft, pop the cubed pieces into a 300°F oven for 15 minutes. Let cool completely before using.
- If your cooker doesn't have a low pressure setting, cook at high pressure for 20 minutes instead.

9. Remove the pan and steam rack and let cool on the rack for at least 20 minutes. If desired, sprinkle sugar on top and broil for 2 to 3 minutes, until lightly browned on top.

10. Serve warm or at room temperature topped with raspberry sauce. Store leftovers in the fridge in an airtight container for up to 3 days.

8 quart: Make as written

NOTES

Brownie Pie with Peanut Butter Swirl

Serves 6

Prep Time: 10 minutes | **Cook Time:** 23 minutes | **Total Time:** 50 minutes

If you like your brownies fudgy, then look no further. Somewhere in between a chocolate fudge pie and a gooey brownie, this dessert is easy to whip up. A swirl of peanut butter on top makes it extra special.

6 tablespoons unsalted butter, melted

1 cup granulated sugar

$1/3$ cup unsweetened cocoa powder

2 eggs

2 tablespoons coffee or espresso, room temperature

1 teaspoon vanilla extract

1 cup all-purpose flour

1 teaspoon baking powder

½ teaspoon salt

½ cup semi or bittersweet chocolate chips (mini or regular)

$1/3$ cup smooth peanut butter

1 tablespoon powdered sugar

1. Add the steam rack to the pot and 1¼ cups water. Grease a 7-inch cheesecake pan or line a 7-inch baking pan with parchment. If needed, create a sling (see page xv).

2. Combine the melted butter, sugar, and cocoa powder in a medium mixing bowl and whisk well. Add the eggs and whisk. Add the coffee and vanilla and whisk.

3. Add the flour, baking powder, and salt and whisk to combine. Mix in the chocolate chips. Pour into the prepared pan and spread to the edges.

4. Warm the peanut butter just until runny in a microwave or double boiler. Add the powdered sugar and mix.

5. Drop in spoonfuls on top of the brownie batter. Use the tip of the spoon to swirl the peanut butter back and forth in one direction and then the other, not mixing it into the brownie batter too much.

6. Cover with aluminum foil and place on the steam rack. Secure the lid.

7. Cook at high pressure for 23 minutes and use a natural release for 10 minutes followed by a quick release.

8. Carefully remove the pan and remove the foil. The brownie should be cooked through but moist. Let cool for a few minutes before removing from the pan. Let cool to room temperature before serving.

9. Store leftovers in an airtight container at room temperature for up to 3 days.

8 quart: Make as written

Ginger Pumpkin Pie

Serves 6

Prep Time: 10 minutes | **Cook Time:** 30 minutes | **Total Time:** 1 hour

Free up your oven for Thanksgiving sides or easily whip up a fall dessert with this Instant Pot pumpkin pie. Fresh ginger adds a nice zip without making it too spicy.

Crust:

1 cup gingersnap crumbs
   (about 4.4 ounces)

4 tablespoons unsalted butter,
   melted

1 tablespoon brown sugar,
   packed

¼ teaspoon salt

Filling:

1⅓ cups pumpkin purée

1 egg

1 egg yolk

½ cup granulated sugar

2 tablespoons finely grated
   fresh ginger

1 teaspoon ground cinnamon

⅛ teaspoon ground cloves

1 pinch ground nutmeg
   (optional)

¼ teaspoon salt

1 cup evaporated milk or half-
   and-half

Note:
- If you don't have
  gingersnaps, use graham
  cracker crumbs and ½
  teaspoon ground ginger.
- Gluten-free cookie crumbs
  can be substituted.

1. Add the steam rack to the pot and 1¼ cups water. Grease a 7-inch cheesecake pan or line a 7-inch baking pan with parchment. If needed, create a sling (see page xv).

2. To make the crust, combine the gingersnap crumbs, melted butter, brown sugar, and salt in a medium bowl. Mix well.

3. Press the mixture into the bottom of the pan and partway up the sides, creating a well-packed and even layer. Place in the freezer while you make the filling. Optional step: for a crispier crust, bake for 10 minutes in a preheated 375°F instead of freezing. Let cool completely.

4. To make the filling, combine the pumpkin purée, egg, egg yolk, sugar, ginger, cinnamon, clove, nutmeg, and salt in a medium mixing bowl. Whisk until completely combined. Add the evaporated milk and whisk until combined.

5. Pour on top of the prepared crust. Cover with aluminum foil and place on the steam rack. Secure the lid.

6. Cook at high pressure for 30 minutes and use a natural release for 10 minutes followed by a quick release.

7. Carefully remove the pan and remove the foil. The pie should be slightly wiggly in the middle and solid around the sides. Let cool to room temperature.

8. If using a cheesecake pan, run a knife around the edge of the pie and remove by pushing up the bottom and removing the sides of the pan.

9. The pie can be served at room temperature or, for a firmer texture, chill for a few hours. Store leftovers in the fridge in an airtight container for up to 3 days.

Gluten-free option | 8 quart: Make as written

Mini Sweet Potato Pies

Serves 4

Prep Time: 10 minutes | **Cook Time:** 15 minutes | **Total Time:** 45 minutes

A Southern classic, sweet potato pies aren't just for the holidays. Made in mini size, you can have them any night of the week. Make with or without a crust and top with toasted marshmallows or whipped cream.

Crust (optional):
½ cup gingersnap or graham cracker crumbs (about 2.2 ounces)
2 tablespoons unsalted butter, melted

Filling:
2 tablespoons unsalted butter, softened (plus extra for greasing ramekins)
$1/3$ cup brown sugar, packed
1 egg, beaten
½ teaspoon vanilla extract
1 cup sweet potato purée, packed (about 1 extra-large or 2 small sweet potatoes)
½ teaspoon ground cinnamon
¼ teaspoon ground ginger
¼ teaspoon salt
$1/3$ cup half-and-half or evaporated milk
1 heaping cup mini marshmallows (optional, or whipped cream)

1. Add the steam rack to the pot and 1¼ cups water. Grease four 6- or 7-ounce ramekins or half-pint mason jars.

2. If making with crust, mix the cookie crumbs and melted butter in a small bowl and press equal amounts into each ramekin. Place in the freezer while you make the filling.

3. To make the filling, beat together the butter and brown sugar with an electric mixer in a medium mixing bowl. Add the egg and vanilla and beat. Add the sweet potato, cinnamon, ginger, and salt and beat. Add the half-and-half and beat until well combined.

4. Spoon an equal amount of batter into each ramekin. Cover each with aluminum foil and place on the steam rack. Secure the lid.

5. Cook at high pressure for 15 minutes and use a natural release for 10 minutes followed by a quick release.

6. Carefully remove the ramekins and remove the foil. The pies should be solid. Let cool to room temperature. If not serving right away, store in the fridge until ready to serve.

7. Top with each with a handful of mini marshmallows (if using) and toast with a brûlée torch or under a hot broiler. Or top with whipped cream.

Notes:
- To cook the sweet potatoes in the Instant Pot: Add 1 cup of water to the pot and add a steam basket or the steam rack. Cut the potatoes in half lengthwise and stack them crisscrossed on the basket. Cook at high pressure for 12 minutes and use a controlled release. Let cool before removing the skins and mashing.
- Gluten-free cookie crumbs can be substituted or the crust can be omitted altogether.

Gluten-free option
3 quart: Cook in batches | 8 quart: Make as written

Matcha Crème Brûlée

Serves 1

Prep Time: 10 minutes | **Cook Time:** 4 minutes | **Total Time:** 30 minutes, plus chill time

It's nearly impossible to make most desserts for one, but here's an easy, decadent treat just for you. This recipe is very easily tweaked—double or triple it for two or three servings, leave out the matcha for a plain crème brûlée, or leave off the sugar topping for a simple custard. Should you choose to include it, the matcha adds a beautiful tea flavor and a light green hue.

1 egg yolk

1 tablespoon granulated sugar plus 1 teaspoon, for the top

½ teaspoon matcha powder

¼ teaspoon vanilla extract

1 pinch salt

⅓ cup heavy cream

1 tablespoon whole milk

Notes:

- To make vanilla crème brûlée, omit the matcha.
- Double or triple this recipe for 2 or 3 servings. Keep the cook time the same.

1. Add the steam rack to the pot and 1¼ cups water.

2. In a small mixing bowl, add the egg yolk, 1 tablespoon sugar, matcha, vanilla, and salt. Whisk together until well mixed.

3. Add the heavy cream and whole milk and whisk until combined.

4. Strain the custard into a 5- or 6-ounce ramekin. Cover with aluminum foil. Place on the steam rack and secure the lid.

5. Cook at low pressure for 4 minutes and use a natural release. The custards should jiggle but not be liquid.

6. Carefully remove from the pot and remove the foil. Let cool to room temperature. If needed, use a paper towel to gently dab away any moisture sitting on top. Chill in the refrigerator, uncovered, for at least 4 hours.

7. When ready to serve, sprinkle with a teaspoon of sugar and tap all around to distribute evenly.

8. Use a kitchen torch to toast the sugar, moving the ramekin constantly to brown evenly and avoid burning. Alternatively, place the ramekins directly under a hot broiler and toast until browned. Serve immediately.

Gluten-free
3 quart: Make as written | 8 quart: Make as written

Mini Flans

Serves 3

Prep Time: 15 minutes | **Cook Time:** 9 minutes | **Total Time:** 45 minutes, plus chill time

Mini flans, also known as crème caramels, are a delightful warm-weather dessert. Smooth and creamy with a caramel sauce that cooks along with the custard, they'll wow any guest. If you're doubling this recipe, cook them in batches, and move quickly with the caramel or it will harden in the pan.

Caramel:

½ cup granulated sugar

2 tablespoons water

¼ teaspoon Kosher or sea salt

Custard:

1 egg

2 egg yolks

3 tablespoons granulated sugar

1 pinch salt

½ cup milk

½ cup heavy cream

1 teaspoon vanilla extract

1. Add the steam rack to the pot and 1¼ cups water.

2. To make the caramel, add the sugar and water to a small saucepan. Stir over medium heat until the sugar dissolves and stop stirring. Turn the heat up to medium-high and bring to a boil. Swirl occasionally (don't stir) and cook for 3 to 5 minutes, until golden brown in color. Moving quickly, add the salt and swirl.

3. Remove from the heat and pour an equal amount into the bottom of three 5- or 6-ounce ramekins. Set aside to cool and harden.

4. To make the custard, add the egg, egg yolks, sugar, and salt to a small mixing bowl. Whisk together until well mixed.

5. Add the milk and heavy cream to a small saucepan over medium-low heat. Barely bring to a simmer, stirring to prevent scorching. Remove from the heat.

6. Slowly add the hot milk mixture into the egg mixture while whisking. Add the vanilla and mix until combined.

7. Strain the custard into the ramekins on top of the caramel. Cover each with aluminum foil. Place on the steam rack and secure the lid.

8. Cook at high pressure for 9 minutes and use a natural release. The custards should jiggle but not be liquid.

9. Carefully remove from the pot and remove the foil. Let cool to room temperature. Loosely cover and transfer to the refrigerator and chill for at least 4 hours or overnight.

Recipe continued on page 68

10. When ready to serve, run a thin knife around the edge of a flan. Carefully invert over a plate. Tilt slightly to the side, if needed, to dislodge. Pour the caramel from the ramekin over the flan. Repeat with remaining flans. Serve immediately.

11. Store leftovers in the fridge in an airtight container for up to 1 day.

Gluten-free
3 quart: Make as written | 8 quart: Make as written

NOTES

Spiced Chocolate Flan

Serves 6–8

Prep Time: 25 minutes | **Cook Time:** 20 minutes | **Total Time:** 1 hour, 15 minutes, plus chill time

Dark chocolate, cinnamon spice, and rich caramel all work together to make this flan special. The chocolate forms a thin layer, giving this flan an extra sophisticated look. Don't walk away when making the caramel—it goes from perfect to burnt in the blink of an eye. Clean your sticky saucepan by soaking with very hot water.

¾ cup sugar

¼ cup water

2 cups whole milk

2 cinnamon sticks

1 ounce unsweetened chocolate, chopped

2 large eggs

4 large egg yolks

1 (14-ounce) can sweetened condensed milk

1 teaspoon vanilla extract

¼ teaspoon salt

1. Add the steam rack to the pot and 1¼ cups water. Prepare a 7-inch baking pan.

2. To make the caramel, add the sugar and water to a small saucepan. Stir over medium heat until the sugar dissolves and stop stirring. Turn the heat up to medium-high and bring to a boil. Swirl occasionally (don't stir) and cook for 5 to 8 minutes, until golden brown in color.

3. Immediately pour the caramel into the baking dish before it solidifies. Turn the pan to coat the bottom. Let cool for at least 5 minutes.

4. Make the custard. Add the milk and cinnamon sticks to a medium saucepan. Heat over medium-low heat, stirring occasionally, until the milk is steaming but not boiling. Remove from the heat and remove the cinnamon sticks. Add the chocolate and stir until melted and no large pieces remain.

5. Add the eggs, egg yolks, sweetened condensed milk, vanilla, and salt to a medium mixing bowl. Whisk together until well mixed.

6. Very slowly pour the hot milk and chocolate mixture into the egg mixture while whisking vigorously. Take your time or you'll end up with scrambled eggs.

7. Strain the custard into the pan on top of the caramel. Cover with aluminum foil. Place on the steam rack and secure the lid.

8. Cook at high pressure for 20 minutes and use a natural release. The flan should jiggle but not be liquid.

Recipe continued on page 70

9. Carefully remove from the pot and remove the foil. Let cool to room temperature. Chill, uncovered, for at least 4 hours or overnight.

10. When ready to serve, remove from the fridge 20 to 30 minutes before serving. Run a thin knife around the edge of the flan. Carefully invert over a plate. Tilt slightly to the side if needed to dislodge. Pour the caramel from the pan over the flan. Serve immediately.

11. Store leftovers in the fridge in an airtight container for up to 1 day.

Gluten-free
3 quart: Make as written | 8 quart: Make as written

NOTES

Dark Chocolate Pudding

Serves 3–4

Prep Time: 10 minutes | **Cook Time:** 5 minutes | **Total Time:** 30 minutes, plus chill time

Smooth and oh-so-chocolatey, this pudding is egg-free and gluten-free, and can easily be made vegan by using nondairy milk. It will keep in the fridge for a few days, making it a great make-ahead dessert.

1½ cups nondairy milk or milk

2 ounces dark chocolate, chopped (or chocolate chips)

1 teaspoon vanilla extract

¼ cup cocoa powder

¼ cup brown sugar, packed

2 tablespoons cornstarch

1 pinch salt

1. Add the steam rack to the pot and 1¼ cups water.

2. Add the milk to a small saucepan over medium-low heat. Heat until small bubbles start to form on the surface (but do not boil) and remove from the heat. Add the chocolate and stir until melted. Add the vanilla.

3. In a small mixing bowl, add the cocoa, brown sugar, cornstarch, and salt and whisk until well mixed.

4. Add the hot chocolate mixture to the cocoa mixture slowly, whisking until well mixed.

5. Pour an equal amount into three 6- or 7-ounce ramekins or half-pint jars. Cover each with aluminum foil. Place on the steam rack and secure the lid.

6. Cook at low pressure for 5 minutes. Use a natural release for 5 minutes followed by a quick release. The puddings should jiggle but not be liquid.

7. Carefully remove from the pot and let cool, covered, for 30 minutes. If you like skin on your pudding, remove the foil.

8. Cover and transfer to the refrigerator. Chill for at least 4 hours before serving. Store leftovers in the fridge for up to 3 days.

Gluten-free | Vegan
3 quart: Make as written | 8 quart: Make as written

White Chocolate Pots de Crème

Serves 2–4

Prep Time: 10 minutes | **Cook Time:** 6 minutes | **Total Time:** 35 minutes, plus chill time

Planning a nice night in? Use your Instant Pot to make a sweet and creamy dessert that's especially tasty topped with berries, but any fresh fruit will do. This recipe makes a generous dessert for two or a pair of shareable desserts for four.

1 egg
1 egg yolk
2 tablespoons granulated sugar
1 pinch salt
¾ cup heavy cream
3 ounces white chocolate
Fresh berries, for serving

1. Add the steam rack to the pot and 1¼ cups water.

2. In a medium mixing bowl, add the egg, egg yolk, sugar, and salt. Whisk together until well mixed.

3. Add the heavy cream to a small saucepan over medium-low heat. Bring to a simmer, stirring to prevent scorching.

4. Very slowly add the hot cream to the egg mixture, whisking vigorously the entire time. Add the chocolate and stir gently until melted and mixed.

5. Divide the custard between two 6- or 7-ounce ramekins or half-pint mason jars and cover each with aluminum foil. Place on the steam rack and secure the lid.

6. Cook at high pressure for 6 minutes and use a natural release. The custards should be solid.

7. Carefully remove from the pot and remove the foil. Let cool to room temperature. Cover and refrigerate at least 4 hours or overnight.

8. Top with fresh berries before serving.

Gluten-free
3 quart: Make as written | 8 quart: Make as written

Amaretto-Cherry Rice Pudding

Serves 4

Prep Time: 10 minutes | **Cook Time:** 10 minutes | **Total Time:** 45 minutes

Cherries and almonds are a flavor match made in heaven. Just a touch of amaretto liqueur adds the sweet almond flavor in this recipe, but it can be swapped for almond extract in a pinch. Just add ½ teaspoon of extract when you add the nutmeg.

½ cup short or medium-grain white rice, rinsed and drained well

3 cups whole milk

⅓ cup granulated sugar

1 pinch salt

1 cup fresh sweet cherries, or frozen cherries thawed and drained

2 tablespoons amaretto liqueur

1 large egg, room temperature, beaten

1 pinch ground nutmeg

Slivered almonds, for garnish (optional)

1. Add the rice, milk, sugar, and salt to the pot. Whisk together and secure the lid.

2. Cook at high pressure for 10 minutes and use a natural release.

3. Meanwhile, stem and pit the cherries, cutting them in half. Combine the cut cherries with the amaretto in a small bowl, tossing to coat. Let sit and toss again every 5 to 10 minutes.

4. Once done pressure cooking, the rice should be cooked through. Don't worry if it looks lumpy. Whisk the cooked rice and milk mixture well to break up any clumps.

5. Temper the egg by slowly adding ½ cup of the hot milky rice to the egg while whisking constantly. Add the mixture back to the pot slowly, whisking the whole time.

6. Turn the sauté function on medium. Add the nutmeg and cherries with amaretto. Stir for a few minutes until the mixture is simmering and starting to thicken up. Turn off the pot.

7. Remove the pot and allow the rice pudding to cool for a few minutes. It will thicken greatly as it sits.

8. Serve warm or cool topped with slivered almonds (if using). Store leftovers in the fridge in an airtight container for up to 3 days.

Gluten-free
3 quart: Make as written | 8 quart: Make as written (can be doubled)

Bourbon Cinnamon Raisin Brown Rice Pudding

Serves 4

Prep Time: 5 minutes | **Cook Time:** 35 minutes | **Total Time:** 1 hour, 10 minutes

Looking for something sweet without a boatload of guilt? Brown rice pudding has added fiber, and this version is vegan to boot—no dairy or eggs required. Another nondairy milk can be used, but the results may not be as creamy. It's best served within an hour or two of making since brown rice can toughen up in the fridge.

¾ cup short-grain brown rice, rinsed and drained well

1 (13.5-ounce) can coconut milk

²/₃ cup water

¼ cup brown sugar, packed

1 pinch salt

1 tablespoon bourbon

1 teaspoon ground cinnamon

½ teaspoon vanilla extract

¼ cup raisins

1. Add the rice, coconut milk, water, brown sugar, and salt to the pot. Whisk together and secure the lid.

2. Cook at high pressure for 35 minutes and use a natural release.

3. The rice should be cooked through and most of the liquid absorbed. Add the bourbon, cinnamon, and vanilla. Whisk the cooked rice mixture well until creamy. Stir in the raisins.

4. Allow the rice pudding to cool for a few minutes. Serve warm.

Gluten-free | Vegan
3 quart: Make as written | 8 quart: Make as written

Coconut Sticky Rice with Mango

Serves 4–5

Prep Time: 15 minutes | **Cook Time:** 13 minutes | **Total Time:** 1 hour, 10 minutes

Mango sticky rice is a classic Thai treat. Sticky rice has a unique, glutenous texture that's fun to eat—find it at Asian markets along with a wide variety of rice. Shake the coconut milk well before opening the can.

---

1 cup Thai sticky rice (sometimes called sweet rice)

²/₃ cup water

1¼ cup coconut milk (canned, not low fat)

¼ cup granulated or raw sugar

¼ teaspoon salt

1 teaspoon cornstarch

2 medium ripe mangos or 1 large mango, peeled and diced

2 tablespoon toasted coconut flakes (optional)

1. Add the steam rack to the pot and 1¼ cups water.

2. Rinse the sticky rice well and drain.

3. In a heatproof bowl or container that fits in the pot, add the drained rice and ²/₃ cup water. Place on the steam rack and secure the lid.

4. Cook at high pressure for 13 minutes and use a natural release for 10 minutes followed by a quick release. The rice should be cooked through.

5. Meanwhile, add the coconut milk, sugar, and salt to a medium saucepan. Heat over medium-low heat, stirring, just until the sugar dissolves.

6. Remove the bowl or container from the pot and pour half of the coconut milk mixture over the rice. Let sit for 20 to 30 minutes to let the liquid soak into the rice. Cover the remaining coconut milk mixture and set aside.

7. Once the coconut milk has soaked into the rice, place the saucepan back over low heat.

8. Add the cornstarch to a small bowl. Add 2 tablespoons of the warm coconut milk mixture to the cornstarch and mix well until all the cornstarch has dissolved. Add the mixture to the saucepan.

9. Increase the heat to medium and bring the sauce to a simmer while stirring. Simmer for 1 minute, or until the sauce has thickened.

10. Plate the sticky rice and top with sauce. Serve immediately with fresh mango on the side. Sprinkle with coconut flakes (if using).

Gluten-free | Vegan
3 quart: Make as written | 8 quart: Make as written

Tiramisu Rice Pudding

Serves 6–8

Prep Time: 10 minutes | **Cook Time:** 10 minutes | **Total Time:** 45 minutes

The flavors of tiramisu—espresso, cocoa, a touch of booze—are also perfectly suited for rice pudding. For a little crunch, sprinkle the top with crumbled biscotti or crisp amaretto cookies.

1 cup short- or medium-grain white rice, rinsed and drained well

5–6 cups whole milk

²/₃ cup granulated sugar

¼ teaspoon salt

2 large eggs, room temperature, beaten

2 ounces (2 shots) espresso

1 tablespoon dark rum (optional)

1 teaspoon vanilla extract

3 tablespoons unsweetened cocoa powder

Note:
- Make it with no added sugar by using a sugar substitute. Follow the sugar replacement instructions on the box.

1. Add the rice, 5 cups of milk, sugar, and salt to the pot. Whisk together and secure the lid.

2. Cook at high pressure for 10 minutes and use a natural release.

3. The rice should be cooked through. Don't worry if it looks lumpy. Whisk the cooked rice and milk mixture well to break up any clumps.

4. Temper the eggs by slowly adding 1 cup of the hot milky rice to the eggs while whisking constantly. Add the mixture back to the pot slowly, whisking the whole time.

5. Turn the sauté function on medium. Whisk for a few minutes until the mixture is simmering and starting to thicken up. Turn off the pot. Add the espresso, rum (if using), and vanilla and mix well.

6. Remove the pot and allow the rice pudding to cool for a few minutes. It will thicken greatly as it sits. If serving chilled, stir in an additional cup of milk before chilling.

7. Serve warm or cool topped with a dusting of cocoa powder. Store leftovers in the fridge in an airtight container for up to 3 days.

Gluten-free | No-added-sugar option
3 quart: Halve the recipe | 8 quart: Make as written

Sauces

Dulce de Leche 83
Grapefruit-Ginger Curd 85
Lime Curd 86

Dulce de Leche

Serves 6

Prep Time: 5 minutes | **Cook Time:** 35 minutes | **Total Time:** 1 hour, 30 minutes, plus cooling time

Dulce de leche is an indulgent caramel sauce that's good on pretty much everything, but it's messy to make on the stove. Luckily, you can make it in a pressure cooker with very little effort. Double or even triple this recipe if you like—just make sure the cans will all fit on the steam rack in your size cooker without touching.

1 (14-ounce) can sweetened condensed milk

½ teaspoon vanilla extract (optional)

Up to ½ teaspoon sea salt (optional)

1. Add the steam rack to the pot.

2. Remove the label from the can of sweetened condensed milk. Open the can, leaving the milk inside the can.

3. Cover the can tightly with aluminum foil. Place on the steam rack. Add enough water to come halfway up the can. Secure the lid.

4. Cook at high pressure for 35 minutes and use a natural release. This will take up to 30 minutes.

5. Carefully remove the can (it will be hot). It should look caramel-colored and thick. Let cool, covered, for 30 minutes.

6. Scoop out into a small mixing bowl and add vanilla and/or salt (if using). Whisk or beat with an electric mixer until very creamy.

7. Store in an airtight container in the refrigerator for up to 2 weeks.

Gluten-free
3 quart: Make as written | 8 quart: Make as written

Grapefruit-Ginger Curd

Serves 10

Prep Time: 10 minutes | **Cook Time:** 12 minutes | **Total Time:** 45 minutes, plus chill time

Sweet and tart with a hint of ginger spice, this curd is great to slather on cakes and scones, or to swirl into your yogurt. It makes a nice gift in a pretty jar and keeps for a couple of weeks in the fridge. Add more ginger if you like spice.

---

5 tablespoons unsalted butter, softened

¾ cup granulated sugar

2 teaspoons finely grated grapefruit zest

1 teaspoon finely grated lemon zest

¼ teaspoon salt

4 eggs

2 egg yolks

¾ cup fresh grapefruit juice, strained

¼ cup fresh lemon juice, strained

1 (1-inch) piece fresh ginger, peeled and finely grated

Notes:
- Make it with no added sugar by using a sugar substitute. Follow the sugar replacement instructions on the box.

1. Add the steam rack to the pot and 1¼ cups water.

2. Add the butter, sugar, grapefruit zest, lemon zest, and salt to a blender, food processor, or a medium mixing bowl. Process or whisk until well mixed. Add the eggs and egg yolks and mix until well blended. Scrape down the sides.

3. Add the grapefruit juice, lemon juice, and ginger, and process or whisk just until well mixed. The mixture might look curdled, but that's okay.

4. Add the mixture to a 7-inch by 3-inch tempered glass container/bowl and cover tightly with aluminum foil. (To make in jars or ramekins, see the Lime Curd recipe on page 86.) Place on the steam rack and secure the lid.

5. Cook at high pressure for 12 minutes and use a natural release for 15 minutes followed by a quick release.

6. Carefully remove the bowl. The mixture may once again look curdled, but that's still okay. Mix vigorously with a whisk until smooth. Cover and let cool for 30 minutes.

7. Chill in the refrigerator in a covered container for at least a few hours before serving. If a smoother consistency is desired, push through a fine-mesh strainer. The curd will keep for 2 weeks in the fridge.

Gluten-free | No-added-sugar option
8 quart: Make as written

Lime Curd

Serves 10

Prep Time: 10 minutes | **Cook Time:** 9 minutes | **Total Time:** 45 minutes, plus chill time

Good, fresh limes will make this recipe sing. If you have access to key limes, use them, but any sour limes will do. Try it on top of pound cake or layered with whipped cream in a trifle.

5 tablespoons unsalted butter, softened
1 cup granulated sugar
2 teaspoons finely grated lime zest
¼ teaspoon salt
2 eggs
3 egg yolks
¾ cup lime juice, strained

Notes:

- Make it with no added sugar by using a sugar substitute. Follow the sugar replacement instructions on the box.

1. Add the steam rack to the pot and 1¼ cups water.

2. Add the butter, sugar, zest, and salt to a blender, food processor, or medium mixing bowl. Process or whisk until well mixed. Add the eggs and egg yolks and mix until well blended. Scrape down the sides.

3. Add the lime juice and process or whisk just until well mixed. The mixture might look curdled, but that's okay. If the mixture is very foamy from blending, let sit for a few minutes before cooking.

4. Add the mixture to 4 half-pint jars or four 6- or 7-ounce ramekins, not filling over two-thirds full. (To make in a single large container, see the Grapefruit-Ginger Curd recipe on page 85.) Cover each tightly with aluminum foil. Place on the steam rack and secure the lid.

5. Cook at high pressure for 9 minutes and use a natural release for 15 minutes followed by a quick release.

6. Carefully remove the jars. Use a fork to stir well until nice and creamy, careful not to burn yourself on the hot jars. Cover and let cool for 30 minutes.

7. Chill in the refrigerator in a covered container for at least a few hours before serving. The curd will keep for 2 weeks.

Gluten-free | No-added-sugar option
3 quart: Cook in batches | 8 quart: Make as written

Acknowledgments

Writing this book would have been much harder and decidedly less fun without my group of recipe testers. Many thanks to Lillian, Marion, Sara, Keri, Whitney, and Mike for your invaluable feedback and support. And recipe test after recipe test, someone had to eat all of these desserts. Heartfelt thanks to my husband, Dan, for happily tasting everything and giving thoughtful feedback, and for hauling desserts to work to share with coworkers. Thanks to the crew of *Mixed-ish* and my fantastic trivia team (Emily, Joe, Peter, and Joel) for tasting dessert after dessert. It's a hard job, but someone's gotta do it. Thank you to my ever-optimistic but always realistic agent, Danielle Chiotti, and thanks to my encouraging and thoughtful editor, Nicole Frail.

About the Author

Laurel Randolph is a best-selling cookbook author and recipe developer. Her first cookbook, *The Instant Pot Electric Pressure Cooker Cookbook*, was released in 2016 and has sold over half a million copies to date. Her second cookbook, *The Instant Pot No-Pressure Cookbook*, was released in May 2018. Laurel has written for *EatingWell, Eaten Magazine, The Spruce, Los Angeles Magazine, Paste Magazine*, and more. She is based in Los Angeles.

Conversion Chart

Metric and Imperial Conversions

(These conversions are rounded for convenience)

Ingredient	Cups/Tablespoons/ Teaspoons	Ounces	Grams/Milliliters
Butter	1 cup/ 16 tablespoons/ 2 sticks	8 ounces	230 grams
Cream cheese	1 tablespoon	0.5 ounce	14.5 grams
Cornstarch	1 tablespoon	0.3 ounce	8 grams
Flour, all-purpose	1 cup/1 tablespoon	4.5 ounces/0.3 ounce	125 grams/8 grams
Flour, whole wheat	1 cup	4 ounces	120 grams
Fruit, dried	1 cup	4 ounces	120 grams
Fruits or veggies, chopped	1 cup	5 to 7 ounces	145 to 200 grams
Fruits or veggies, pureed	1 cup	8.5 ounces	245 grams
Honey, maple syrup, or corn syrup	1 tablespoon	0.75 ounce	20 grams
Liquids: cream, milk, water, or juice	1 cup	8 fluid ounces	240 milliliters
Oats	1 cup	5.5 ounces	150 grams
Salt	1 teaspoon	0.2 ounce	6 grams
Spices: cinnamon, cloves, ginger, or nutmeg (ground)	1 teaspoon	0.2 ounce	5 milliliters
Sugar, brown, firmly packed	1 cup	7 ounces	200 grams
Sugar, white	1 cup/1 tablespoon	7 ounces/0.5 ounce	200 grams/12.5 grams
Vanilla extract	1 teaspoon	0.2 ounce	4 grams

Index

Additional Notes

Additional Notes

Additional Notes

Additional Notes

Additional Notes

Additional Notes

Additional Notes

Additional Notes

Additional Notes

Additional Notes

Additional Notes

Additional Notes

Additional Notes

Additional Notes

Also Available

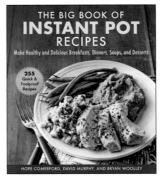

MASTERING THE INSTANT VORTEX PLUS

A Practical Guide to the 7-in-1 Air Fryer and All Its Functions

75 Quick and Easy Tips for Home Cooks!

JAMES O. FRAIOLI, James Beard Award Winner

MASTERING THE INSTANT POT

A Practical Guide to Using "The Greatest Kitchen Tool of All Time"

125 Quick and Easy Tips for Cooks

JENNY DORSEY
Author of *Air Frying for Everyone and One Pot Meals*

By the *New York Times* bestselling author

FIX-IT and FORGET-IT

A **$47.85** VALUE!

BOX SET

FIX-IT and FORGET-IT Cookbook

FIX-IT and FORGET-IT Christmas Cookbook

FIX-IT and FORGET-IT 5-ingredient favorites

PHYLLIS GOOD

NEW YORK TIMES BESTSELLING SERIES

FIX-IT and FORGET-IT COOKING FOR TWO

150 SMALL-BATCH SLOW COOKER RECIPES

HOPE COMERFORD

FIX-IT and FORGET-IT SLOW COOKER

Champion Recipes

BY THE *New York Times* BESTSELLING AUTHOR!

450 OF OUR VERY BEST RECIPES

PHYLLIS GOOD

By The *New York Times* bestselling author

FIX-IT and FORGET-IT® BIG COOKBOOK

1400 Best Slow Cooker Recipes!

Phyllis Pellman Good

NEW YORK TIMES BESTSELLING SERIES

FIX-IT and FORGET-IT BIG BOOK OF KETO RECIPES

275 HEALTHY **SLOW COOKER & INSTANT POT** FAVORITES

225 BONUS OVEN, STOVETOP, AND GRILLING RECIPES!

EDITED BY HOPE COMERFORD

FROM THE EDITOR OF THE *NEW YORK TIMES* BESTSELLING FIX-IT AND FORGET-IT SERIES

Welcome Home Harvest Cookbook

Hope Comerford

INCLUDES **450** RECIPES

QUICK-AND-EASY FARM-TO-TABLE DINNERS AND DESSERTS